Succeeding and Failing in Australian Environment Policy

Kathleen Mackie with Stephen Saunders

Brou Lake Publishing

Published by Brou Lake Publishing

E: kathmackie@gmail.com or stephen@saunders.net

First published in 2018

Copyright © 2018 Kathleen Mackie and Stephen Saunders

ISBN: 978-0-646-98234-2

A catalogue record for this book is available from the National Library of Australia

Typesetting by Power of Words. Clontarf Queensland 4019

E: jennifer@jenniferlancaster.com.au

Printed in Australia by IngramSpark

Cover photo by Kathleen Mackie:

Golden everlastings (*Xerochrysum bracteatum*) at Kings Park WA, 2016

Authors and Acknowledgements

The author Kathleen Mackie made a 22-year career in the Australian Public Service (APS) up to 2009, mainly at the Senior Executive Service Level in the federal Department of the Environment. From August 2016 to December 2017, she served as Chief Executive Officer at the Kanyirninpa Jukurrpa organisation, an Indigenous organisation of the Martu people of the Pilbara in Western Australia.

She holds a B.A. (Hons) in Applied Economic Geography from UNSW, an M.A. in Human Geography from the University of Toronto, and a (2015) PhD in Political Science from UNSW. This book is substantially based upon her PhD research.

Acknowledgements for research support are due to UNSW as the scholarship provider, and UNSW supervisors, Dr David Meacheam and Dr Kieran Sharpe. The support of the federal Department of the Environment and the contribution of the 51 present or former Environment officials who agreed to be interviewed are gratefully acknowledged. Professor Stephen Dovers at ANU and Professor Allan McConnell at University of Sydney provided valuable insights on the research.

Kathleen's partner, and editor, Stephen Saunders, also had a long APS career, mainly with the Department of Employment, Education and Training and its equivalents. He holds a B.Sc. (Hons) in Mathematical Statistics from UWA, and an M.A. in Urban Geography from McMaster University, Ontario. He is a former consultant, Canberra Times reviewer, and radio broadcaster.

Contents

Tables, Figures, Illustrations

Introduction

Why do some government policies succeed, when some muddle through, and others spiral into failure? How can we decide what is 'success' and on what basis? Too often, academics study these important questions with little or no access to the frank opinions of influential policy officials in the backroom.

In Australian federal government, the 'Westminster' convention has it that officials advise and ministers decide. The hidden role of officials, striving to craft viable policies and steer them towards success, is not easy to observe in practice or express in theory. This book, however, is based directly on insider interviews with the pivotal federal environment officials.

To set the scene, Chapter 1 takes a longer view of Australian environment policy, traditionally a state responsibility. It introduces the relatively recent federal engagement with environmental policy. On the basis of their scope and environmental impact, 12 federal environment (biodiversity and energy) policies or programs are chosen as the subject of closer examination.

The first, tiny federal Environment Department was only set up in 1971. Labor Environment Minister Richardson drove the Department to greater prominence in the 1980s. The Howard Government's first Environment Minister, Senator Hill, was a Cabinet member, and the portfolio remains a Cabinet member to this day.

Over the 1990s, the Department developed national strategies in biodiversity, forest policy, marine policy, and oceans policy. Senator Hill brokered the *Environment Protection and Biodiversity Conservation (EPBC) Act*. For the first time, the federal environment minister became the main decision-maker on matters of national environmental significance.

The Rudd Government created a separate Department of Climate Change in 2007. During the Global Financial Crisis, the Environment Department received its biggest funding package, including Home Insulation. Albeit with reduced funding, the Department has retained its Cabinet status under the Abbott and Turnbull Governments. It has reabsorbed the climate-change function.

As the Department evolved from the 1970s, it nurtured a skilled and determined generation of environment policy officials. These were the core officials Kathleen Mackie interviewed for her PhD thesis (Mackie, 2015) from the University of New South Wales. Her research was triggered by her own Senior Executive experiences of turmoil inside the Home Insulation Program, which contrasted starkly with earlier positive experiences in developing the Working on Country program.

Chapter 2 discusses the changing theories since the 1950s about the nature of policy success generally. It summarises an extensive literature on the main preconditions or precursors for such success. While this uncovers no single overarching theory readily applicable to environment policy, it is invaluable for structuring the interviews and the interview questions.

Much thinner on the ground is literature about the success or failure of actual or existing policies. The final section of Chapter 2, however, introduces the Marsh and McConnell Framework. That Framework assesses program success or failure along process, programmatic and political dimensions. Although it is fairly recent in origin, it has already been applied fruitfully. In Chapters 3 and 5, it will be re-applied, to check the reasonableness of interviewee ratings of program success and failure.

In the wake of the Home Insulation Program debacle, the research for this book was preoccupied by two key questions. *Do policy officials have a prior sense of whether or not a policy is likely to succeed? What are the key factors likely to drive policy success?*

Chapter 3 establishes the preferred approach to tackle these questions, that is, in-depth and semi-structured interviews with the key environment policymakers. This is supported by reference to publicly available reports and evaluations, plus a closer scrutiny of the 12 programs or policies targeted in Chapter 1.

The 26 male and 25 female interviewees were a representative sample of the senior officials who had occupied key federal environment policy roles over the period 1993-2013. Thirty-one were present or former members of the Senior Executive Service, including all five of the Environment Department Heads (Secretaries) from the period.

Among the target programs, the interviewees would rate Working on Country and Fuel Quality Standards as notable successes. Their most conspicuous failures were the Home Insulation Program and Green Loans.

They generally agreed on which programs were successful, mixed in outcomes, or failed. These assessments generally lined up with those derived externally, by applying the Marsh and McConnell Framework.

The interviewees claimed a strong advance sense of whether or not a policy was going to play out successfully – even if they themselves had not worked on that policy. In Chapter 4, we analyse the most important predictive factors for policy success that the interviewees put forward.

Among prominent factors in the policy literature, they confirmed the importance of engaging with stakeholders, having clear objectives, and knowing the evidence base. In the particular context of environment policy, they played down other prominent factors – adequacy of resources, nature of the policy origins, and clear policy design.

The interviews would emphasise two novel factors – strength of the policy mandate and exercise of policy 'agency'. A capable Environment Minister, like Liberal Senator Hill or Labor Senator Richardson, could extract more from the policy mandate. Policy 'agency' – legitimate but incisive interventions by officials to get a result for the good of the environment – was a critical indicator for policy success.

That being said, the policymakers were mindful that environment policy sits uncomfortably with the dominant economic paradigms. They had become adept at dressing up 'green' environment programs in 'brown' economic and social clothing.

Policy officials pursued strategies such as adding a land-clearing moratorium into Commonwealth-State agreements; invoking certain clauses of the EPBC Act to unlock marine protection policy; and, paying Indigenous workers fair wages to maintain natural and cultural estates on Indigenous and other tenures.

These are actual examples of the unobtrusive 'agency' exercised by seasoned officials, to extract better outcomes from environmental policies that happen to be on the government's agenda. Conversely, the poor outcomes in Home Insulation and Green Loans partly arose from a distinct lack of 'agency', as officials failed to provide frank and timely advice.

Chapter 5 draws up contrasting case studies of Home Insulation and the Sustainable Population Strategy as failed programs, Working on Country and Fuel Quality Standards as successes. This includes worked examples of the practical application of the Marsh and McConnell Framework. All the case studies have postscripts for fresh developments over 2015-17.

Eighteen interviewees failed the Home Insulation Program, but five others rated it successful, on the grounds of its economic stimulus. The Framework sides with the majority, being obliged to take into the account the program's four deaths, dire implementation, failure to meet insulation and environmental objectives, and long years of political fallout.

Home Insulation and Sustainable Population both divided those officials who rated the programs. Both also illustrate the pitfalls of top-down or politically driven policy, where objective evidence tends to be put to one side and the 'agency' of top Departmental officials is stifled.

All the interviewees who rated Working on Country or Fuel Quality thought these programs were successful. The application of the Framework leads to the same conclusions. Both these programs created durable 'templates' that could survive changes of government, and would enable successful program expansion over numbers of years.

As described in Chapter 5, Fuel Quality is a rare case of environment policy that starts from 'first principles' and ticks the boxes for successful policy development found in the literature. As for Working on Country, its core environment objectives travelled under disguise. At the time of inception, there was limited upfront scientific, environmental or health evidence, for its distinctive policy design.

In conclusion, at Chapter 6, we argue for more attention to policy success. While measures of such success can never be totally 'objective', they can be rigorous, and moderate partisan or ideological assessments of policy outcomes. We find the Marsh and McConnell Framework useful for these purposes, and give reasons why it might be extended to highlight the equity (winners and losers) aspects of policy. Though some decry a public service weakened by the rise of outside policy-advice influences, we contend that able officials can still play a critical 'agency' role in generating policy successes, by extension of the tried and tested Westminster principles.

Chapter 1
Setting the Environment Policy Scene

The national or federal environment-policy push that enables this book is of fairly recent origin. Before the 1970s, there was no federal Environment Department and no broad suite of federal environment policies that could have been studied. These developments are considered in the second and third sections of this chapter.

The opening section gives a longer view of Australian environment policy. This includes the conceptual underpinnings, the cultural or economic approaches to the natural environment, and theories or assessments of environment policy outcomes.

1.1 A long view of Australian environment policy

Taking a shorter view from the 1970s or 1980s, the environmental (particularly energy and emissions policy, but also re the natural estate) rollbacks of the Abbott Government from 2013 could be perceived as a major, even ideological, unravelling of sensible or established environment policies.

Taking the longer view from Federation and even beforehand, such rollbacks could be perceived as an unremarkable reversion to our Australian historical norms. In these norms, the unique features of the Australian ecosystems tend to be viewed with detachment or disdain, in a European cultural equation of enthusiastic population growth and continual environmental modification, with scant regard for possible costs down the line.

One trigger for this book is the sparse literature on Australian environmental policy, including success or failure in such policy. In 1992, Walker regretted our consistent lack of attention to the "politics of environmental policy" (Walker, 1992, ix). He remarked on the lack of knowledge of our fragile ecosystems, among scientists and politicians alike. "Ecological systems do not understand political constraints: if critical thresholds are passed, destabilisation is inevitable" (Walker, 1992, 13).

Walker (Walker, 1992, Walker, 1994, Walker and Crowley, 1999, Crowley and Walker, 2012) and later environment policy theorists (Crowley, 2002, Dovers, 2005, Stewart and Jones, 2003, Lindenmayer, 2007, Thomas, 2007, Dovers and Hussey 2013) broadly agree there is a global environmental crisis and Australia faces considerable environment policy challenges. Their conclusion is based on our high level of species endemism, significant share of world biodiversity values (Department of Environment Water Heritage and the Arts, 2010b), high rates of species and habitat loss, high levels of introduced species impacts, and fragile natural environment.

Cataloguing the impacts of population pressure, climate change, habitat and species losses, scientists argue that Australia fails to meet its legislative and international commitments to protect the environment. Lindenmayer (2007, 71) sets out such a case. His prime evidence is Australia's high numbers of extinct and threatened species and its world lead in recent mammal extinctions (Lindenmayer, 2007, xii-xiii). Dovers (2005, 36) argued that environment policy failure in Australia had deepened, to the extent that even official policy statements were now admitting policy shortfalls.

Notable in this regard is the five-yearly State of the Environment (SoE) reporting required under Section 516B of the *Environment Protection and Biodiversity Conservation Act 1999 (EPBC Act 1999)*. SoE has few equivalents among similar OECD nations. After a first SoE Report in 1986, five major SoE reports have emerged since 1996. The report has grown to become a notable scientific, government-backed assessment of Australian environment policy.

The 2011 Committee rests its claim of independence on the use of best available evidence, extensive consultation, and peer-review (State of the Environment 2011 Committee, 2011, 23). It provides 'optimistic' and 'pessimistic' assessments, recognising the contested nature of assessing the state of the environment.

The Committee ventures (State of the Environment 2011 Committee, 2011, 568, 579, 606) that there are increasing risks of population collapses in native species across much of Australia. It confirms the concerning finding of conservation organisations (Fitzsimons et al., 2010, 2) that, based on current trends in Northern Australia, many native mammals will go extinct there in the next ten to 20 years. The delayed 2016 SoE Report offers little fresh comfort. "The main pressures facing the Australian environment today are the same as in 2011," the SoE Committee summarises (Australian Government, 2017, 5) "climate change, land-use change, habitat fragmentation and degradation, and invasive species; and much of Australia's unique environment is declining across a range of aspects and indicators."

Crowley and Walker (2012, 174-175) called this type of ecological decline in the face of continued environment policy efforts "policy failure of the highest order". In Crowley and Walker (2012, 11-20), Walker's essay underscores the ingrained philosophical underpinnings of our "statist developmentalism" as he dubs it. From early colonial times, he notes, settlement laws have required land clearing and encouraged British farming and cropping models that dismissed Indigenous land husbandry and often misfit the terrain at hand.

This state of mind retains a strong 21st century hold, with continuing development ever assumed to be imperative, popular, and advantageous. The 2015 Northern Australia White Paper illustrates the contemporary relevance of Walker's analysis. In the fulfilment of its development model, it urges major damming works, and it demands an unprecedented four or fivefold increase in the region's population by 2060 (Australian Government, 2015, 4). It glosses over environmental constraints, including the specific extinction threat referred to above.

Dovers' (2005, 38) key reasons for environment policy failure are poor understanding of the problems and poor policy processes. Success, he said, would be more in reach if the broader community were included in policy processes, with a more integrated and whole-of-government approach. Dovers (2005, 38, 184) concluded that policy failure would be reduced if 'sustainability' principles were embedded in all policy sectors and agencies, and in the legislative underpinnings.

The concept of 'sustainable' development was nested in the paradigm of economic growth, being an attempt to integrate concern for the environment with economic interests. Dovers defined sustainability as "the ability of human society to persist in the long term in a manner that satisfied human development demands but without threatening the integrity of the natural world" (Dovers, 2005, 7).

Lindenmayer (2007, xiv) defined ecological sustainability in terms of perpetuating ecosystem integrity while continuing to provide resources for use and non-use values. But 'sustainability', he continued, has been so widely abused as to become a weasel word bereft of meaning. In his view, this use of the word elides government's intent to continue to boost economic growth and yet claim action on protecting the environment. In exactly this reflexive sense, the word appeared in the former Labor Government's unwieldy title of the 'Department of Sustainability, Environment, Water, Population and Communities'.

Crowley (2002) and Nevill (2007) observed that the most common approach to Australian environment policy analysis – descriptive case studies – leaves a thirst for better explanations of policy outcomes. Crowley (2002, 485) contended that political scientists had the best critical analysis on offer, when it came to understanding environment policy failure. But Kellow (2009) observed that our environment politics had received limited attention from political scientists. She concluded that many studies of environment policy are of limited theoretical, cross-sectoral, or international comparative, value. There are too many "single-shot case studies" that are usually of a normative tenor (Kellow, 2009, 354-355).

Some environment policy theorists cite the political leaning of the major federal parties as an important influence on the scope for environment policy outcomes. Such claims occur in the works of Economou (1999), Stewart and Hendriks (2008), and Pearse (2007). However, at different times from the 1970s onwards, notable environmental outcomes have been recorded under Liberal *or* Labor (see Tables 1.1 and 1.2 below). Good environmental policies have enjoyed bi-partisan support, as with Working on Country. It is a salient point of this book that the more able environment ministers can make a difference under *either* party.

More subtly, environment theorists have ventured into political analyses of the role of power in resource use decisions (Stewart and Jones, 2003, Walker, 1994). Dryzek's (1987) insights on ecological rationality, Dovers and Hussey (2013) on sustainability, Stewart (2009) on values, and Lindenmayer (2007) on the importance of evidence and science, are wide-ranging analyses of why environment policy is failing.

Typically, environment policy analyses resource-use conflicts in terms of the continuing primacy of development over environment protection (Ajani, 2007, Crace, 2011, Krien, 2010, Wescott, 2009, Yencken and Wilkinson, 2000). In such studies, causes of environment policy failure (over and above the dominance of an economic framework over an ecological perspective) are easy to find. They include insufficient understanding of ecological processes and the importance of biodiversity, lack of political will, short-term electoral cycles, a discount rate that disadvantages future generations, and the primacy of industry interests over conservation interests. The interviewees for this book proved to be well aware of these constraints, and would frame policy accordingly.

In response, Walker (1994), Crowley and Walker (2012), Dovers (2005), and Stewart and Jones (2003) have argued that economic and ecological imperatives need to be rebalanced in new governance models if environment policy failure is to be avoided.

A Machiavellian view of environment policy failure is that of Higgs (2014), whose argument amplifies an earlier analysis found in Beder (2002). Drawing heavily on US and Australian examples, both contend that the deep pockets of the business lobby have invested heavily in free-market public-relations persuasion and outright manipulation in favour of "endless growth on a finite planet", so as to outflank and neutralise the community environmental concerns and environmental re-regulation that were prominent from the 1960s to the 1980s. In a related vein, Pearse (2007) fears that a "greenhouse mafia" with strong backing from the coal and utility industries has tended to subvert Australian greenhouse strategies from the 1990s.

Without denying this pessimistic long-term view in the literature, where Australia's economic and development imperatives repeatedly overrule the application of prudent long-term environmental safeguards, nevertheless it may be said that environment policy successes can be attributed to actions taken by the Federal Government.

The expanded role for the Federal Government *has* led to quantitative improvements in areas such as ozone protection, urban air quality, water quality and fuel quality. It *has* led to significant areas of land and sea being placed under protection through the National Reserve System, national parks, Indigenous Protected Areas and Marine Protected Areas. Iconic areas such as Fraser Island and the Wet Tropics were to some degree protected from unsustainable resource use (although the level of protection is not immutable and may be subject to challenge). In addition, federal interventions have slowed the pace of clearing of native vegetation and native forests (although such measures have proven to be quite vulnerable to rollbacks by the States).

National strategies have been used as overarching frameworks to establish policy agendas new to the Commonwealth, in areas ranging from forest to marine policy. There have been unexpected successes in challenging policy areas, such as the Working on Country program for Indigenous rangers.

These positive environmental outcomes delivered through federal intervention are captured in Tables 1.1 and 1.2 in the next section. They suggest a level of energy and achievement in federal environment policy that is at least a grace note to the "litany of failure" that Crowley and Walker (2012, 7) not unreasonably perceived.

1.2 Federal engagement in Australian environment policy

In dividing up powers between the Australian Government and the six States, the Australian Constitution did not expressly provide for the Commonwealth Parliament to make environment laws. That omission meant that for over half of the 20th century the regulation of most environmental matters, including management of land, coasts, rivers, water and the atmosphere, defaulted to the States (Economou, 1999). The Australian Government's role was largely confined to the environmental consequences of its own actions (Early, 2008, 4).

Right up until the 1970s, the Commonwealth had little direct or consequential role in environmental policy. It had no legislative teeth for environment interventions. Federal environmental policy successes (or failures) simply would not have happened, not on the scale that is to be discussed in this book.

The recent and stronger federal engagement in environment policy may be considered in terms of four related forces in society and politics:

- Responding to community concerns, the Commonwealth increasingly intervened in environmental matters from the 1970s, deploying large grants programs under coherent national legislation.

- In parallel, the Environment Department transformed from a minor office into a substantial Department, whose Minister has held a Cabinet seat ever since 1996.

- Instrumental Environment Ministers, in particular Labor Senator Richardson (1998-90) and Liberal Senator Hill (1996-2001), delivered breakthroughs for biodiversity, energy, marine, water, and Indigenous land management, policy.

- The pressure of minor parties (Democrats and Greens) and independent Senators negotiated political deals that secured big environmental decisions and funding.

These four forces are discussed in turn below.

A coherent approach to national environmental legislation emerges

Federal-versus-State shifts in responsibility for environment policy are a key to understanding the evolution of environment policy at the national level.

From the 1970s to the 1990s, environment issues were not pivotal for the Federal Government. Nevertheless, there were 'spikes' of political activity provoked by intense community concerns over specific sites of high environmental value.

Site-by-site campaigns to save areas of high conservation value shaped government engagement in environment policy. The first major battle was over a small but remarkable Tasmanian glacial lake. In 1971, the Tasmanian Government 'won' that fight, by approving a hydroelectric power dam. But the drowning of Lake Pedder had far-reaching implications for the federal-State division of roles and responsibilities. It spawned an environmental movement and a political party that was to become a third force in federal politics (Department of Environment and Heritage, 2004, 11).

Following Lake Pedder came other high-profile cases to protect iconic areas. Fraser Island in Queensland in 1976, the Franklin River in Tasmania in 1983, and the Wet Tropics rainforests of Northern Queensland in 1988, disrupted the national treatment of environmental matters.

The primary national environment legislation being used in the 1970s was the *Environment Protection (Impact of Proposals) Act 1974 (EPIP Act 1974).* However, this Act only applied to decisions involving the Commonwealth or a Commonwealth authority. The Environment Minister's role was merely advisory. At the time, it was the norm for environment impact assessment legislation to focus on informing decision-makers, rather than say who would be the decision-maker (interviewee comment).

By the 1990s, the use of the *EPIP Act 1974* (and other trade or corporations powers) to protect the environment was becoming (said one of our interviewees) haphazard and ineffectual. The disparate legislation and the unsettling Federal-State tug-of-war over who had legislative control in environmental disputes led to the *EPBC Act 1999.*

The new Act repealed the *EPIP Act 1974* and wrapped in four other pieces of environment legislation. For the first time, the Environment Minister held the primary decision-making role on matters of National Environmental Significance (NES) (Hawke, 2009, 3). The Act continues to be the most significant national environment legislation, while still leaving matters of state, regional or local significance to the States or to local government (Department of the Environment, 2013a).

Under the Act (as at 2015) any proposed action or project requires approval from the Environment Minister if it is likely to have a significant impact on a matter protected by the Act. No person is to take any such 'controlled' action except in accordance with that approval (Early, 2008, 11). The main initial objects of the Act were to:

- provide for the protection of the environment, especially those aspects of the environment that are matters of national environmental significance including threatened species and ecologically significant communities, wetlands and migratory species, world heritage;

- promote ecologically sustainable development (ESD) through the conservation and ecologically sustainable use of natural resources; and

- promote the conservation of biodiversity (Early, 2008, 10).

The EPBC assessment and approval process tries to negotiate conditions to mitigate, offset or avoid those impacts. However, up until mid 2010, only *eight* proposals had ever been rejected outright on the grounds of unacceptable impact on the environment (Department of Environment Water Heritage and the Arts, 2010a, 114). Two more proposals had been rejected outright by November 2013. Trenchant critics regard the Act as a 'fractionated' instrument, conveniently designed to relinquish biodiversity, whenever saving it would threaten development interests.

For example, two interviewees said that the express exclusion of the impact of forestry in Regional Forest Agreement (RFA) areas became problematic, once the RFAs failed to deliver on ecologically sustainable forestry management. Neither has the Act stemmed unsustainable rates of water usage, because water policy is not treated as a matter of NES. The Act itself has not really helped to stem native vegetation clearing, partly because it was designed to operate on a 'challenge' or 'exception' basis. This loophole resurfaced in 2015. Pleas were made for the Act to be invoked to stop large-scale private land clearing of Queensland Gulf country, endorsed just before the Queensland Liberal National Government fell (ABC News, 5 June 2015). Later the same year, (Hunt, 15 October 2015) Minister Hunt re-approved under the Act the Carmichael (Adani) Coal Mine project, supposedly with "36 of the strictest conditions in Australian history".

Table 1.1: Federal environment policy, key events 1970-1991

Liberal Party of Australia (LPA) Gorton (1968–1971) McMahon (1971-72)

| 1970 Nov | First Commonwealth Office of the Environment established, but with no staff. |
| 1971 May | Small Department of Environment, Aborigines and the Arts set up. |

Australian Labor Party (ALP) Whitlam (1972–1975)

1972 Dec	Junior Department of Environment & Conservation set up, 93 staff and $0.2m budget.
1972	United Nations (UN) Conference on the Human Environment (Stockholm Conference).
1972	United Tasmania Group set up, largely to campaign against damming of Lake Pedder.
1972	Lake Pedder in Tasmania flooded by dam for hydro-electricity, despite Federal offer.
1974	*EPIP Act* and *States Grants (Nature Conservation) Act* passed.
1975	*National Parks and Wildlife Conservation Act* enacted and ANP&WS established.
1975 Apr	Department of the Environment renamed – now 230 staff and $13 million budget.

Table 1.1: Federal environment policy, key events 1970-1991 (cont.)

LPA Fraser (1975–1983)

1975	Great Barrier Reef (GBR) declared a Marine Park.
1976	Fraser Island Environmental Inquiry halts sand mining on the island.
1976	The Tasmanian Wilderness Society (later to become The Wilderness Society) set up.
1976	NT Land Rights Act passed.
1977	Ayers Rock declared a National Park and renamed Uluru-Kata Tjuta.
1978	Australian whaling ends.
1979	Logging protests at Terania Creek (NSW) – the first such large, on-site, direct protest.
1979	Kakadu National Park (Stage 1) established.
1981	Kakadu, GBR, and Willandra Lakes Region, inscribed as World Heritage Areas.
1982	World Heritage nomination for Southwest Tasmania.
1982	Rainforest Conservation Society set up, to protect Daintree Rainforest in Queensland.
1982	Blockades and other direct action begin, to prevent damming of the Franklin River.

ALP Hawke (1983–1991)

1983	Sydney Greens register as the first Australian Greens party.
1983	National Conservation Strategy for Australia announced.
1983	SW Tasmania gets World Heritage status, to prevent HEC damming of Franklin River.
1983	Campaign to save the Gordon River from being dammed.
1985	Murray-Darling Basin Ministerial Council established.

Table 1.1: Federal environment policy, key events 1970-1991 (cont.)

ALP Hawke (1983–1991) ...cont'd	
1984	Tasmanian Wilderness Society goes national, as 'The Wilderness Society'.
1986	First national SoE Report published by the Federal Government.
1986	Landcare commences, in Victoria.
1988	Richardson becomes Environment Minister, Qld Wet Tropics declared World Heritage.
1989	Hawke releases Environment Statement, announces bi-partisan 'Decade of Landcare'.
1989	'One Billion Trees' program announced.
1989	Australian Government follows 1987 Montreal Protocol, to ban chlorofluorocarbons.
1991	Federal Government postpones mining at Coronation Hill, NT.

Key source: Appendix B, internal 'History of the Department of Environment and Heritage', (2004)

In its defence, the Act did create a more effective national framework for environment protection than previous Acts. It entrenched ESD principles, with the 'precautionary principle' at the centre of decision-making (Early, 2008, 45). It has been used to stop several proposals that would have degraded environmental values, notably the Traveston Dam proposal in Queensland, the placement of oilrigs in the Great Barrier Reef, and a Victorian Government proposal to allow cattle grazing in the Alps. One of the Abbott Government's environmental rollbacks was a decision for a cattle grazing trial in the Victorian Alps in March 2014 (Hunt, 6 March 2014).

The Act placed the Environment Minister and his Department at the centre of decision-making on matters of National Environmental Significance (NES). An interviewee explained how unusual this was:

> 'One of the key reforms under the Act was that the Environment Minister was the decision-maker rather than just providing advice to line Ministers. If you look at other systems in Australia and overseas, we are either unique, or close to unique, in having the Environment Minister as the decision-maker.'

Despite its weaknesses, the *EPBC Act 1999* is a key piece of armoury at the Federal Government's disposal, giving its Environment Minister considerable discretion. The Act can be used to control the impact of future developments on nationally significant environmental assets. During and since the Abbott Government, concerted efforts to devolve decision making to the States have further weakened the value of the Act as a tool to protect the environment and biodiversity.

The federal Environment Department expands its policy range

At first, the position of the Environment Department was marginal. Its Minister held little sway in Cabinet. There were five different Environment Ministers in the first five 1970s years of the Department.

The slowly expanding size and remit of the Department has tracked the gradually increasing federal engagement in environmental matters. Throughout, the environment function has been merged with and demerged from other functions. These have included water, science, population policy, climate change and energy efficiency, plus minor functions such as housing affordability, communities, home affairs, arts, heritage, sport, tourism and territories. New functions of population and sustainability were added to the Department and its name in 2011. The Abbott Government simply reverted to a 'Department of the Environment', albeit with climate change functions restored, in the Administrative Arrangement Orders of 18 September 2013.

Despite the continuing mergers and changes of function, the Environment Portfolio delivered environmental outcomes from the outset, as summarised in Table 1.1 above.

Under the 1972-75 Whitlam Government, the fledgling Department laid a foundation for future legislative and management action by successive federal governments to protect the environment. This included the first environmental legislation, the *EPIP Act 1974,* the *States Grants (Nature Conservation) Act 1974*, and legislative machinery for the National Parks and Wildlife Service and Australian Heritage Commission (Department of Environment and Heritage, 2004, 12).

Between 1975 and 1981, the Fraser Government halted sand mining on Fraser Island (1976), declared national parks at Uluru (1977) and Kakadu (1979), and listed the Great Barrier Reef as a World Heritage Area (1981).

Table 1.1 concludes with achievements under the Hawke Government of 1983-91. South West Tasmania and the Wet Tropics were granted World Heritage Status, and the Gordon River was preserved. The first State of the Environment Report was published. In 1989, Australia followed the international lead, banning the use of chlorofluorocarbons (CFCs) and thus helping to preserve the ozone layer.

From 1990, the Australian Government, the States and local governments had begun to achieve a more co-operative and orderly approach to national environmental issues, reflected in the 1992 Intergovernmental Agreement on the Environment (IGAE) (Early, 2008, 6). Under the IGAE, all Australian jurisdictions agreed to integrate environmental considerations into decision-making and pursue ESD principles. On the international front, the 1992 Rio Declaration, and in Australia the 1992 National Strategy for Ecologically Sustainable Development (Commonwealth of Australia, December 1992), enshrined the notion of sustainability. Although these documents were only 'aspirational' to begin with, later they acquired force under the *EPBC Act*.

A second phase of federal environment policy from 1992 to 2014 is exhibited in Table 1.2. While Prime Minister Howard declined to ratify the Kyoto Protocol, and secured international agreement to an emissions target 8 per cent *above* 1990 levels, his Government introduced Indigenous Protected Areas in 1996, launched Australia's Oceans Policy and Greenhouse Office in 1998, proclaimed national fuel quality standards in 2002, ramped up Great Barrier Reef protections while establishing the National Water Initiative (2003-04), and introduced Working on Country in 2007.

As per Table 1.2, Australia finally endorsed the Kyoto Protocol during the Rudd-Gillard period of 2007-2013. Said Labor Government announced Caring for our Country and the near $1 billion Biodiversity Fund, but had mixed or negative outcomes with other major environmental initiatives in terms of solar, Green Loans, Home Insulation, and Sustainable Population. Inside its first year, the succeeding Abbott Government committed to remove the carbon tax, 'streamlined' the environmental approvals process, and wound up the Biodiversity Fund.

Table 1.2: Federal environment policy, key events 1992-2014

ALP Keating (1991–1996)	
1992	Intergovernmental Agreement on the Environment signed by Prime Minister, State Premiers, and the Australian Local Government Association.
1992	COAG adopts the final National Strategy for Ecologically Sustainable Development.
1992	Environment Statement released, with a National Reserve Strategy of $11.5m over 4 years.
1992	Decade of Landcare launched.

Table 1.2: Federal environment policy, key events 1992-2014 (cont.)

1992	National Forest Policy Statement signed by all states, except Tasmania, which signed 1995.
1993	Native Title Act proclaimed – base for Indigenous Protected Areas, *Working on Country*.

LPA Howard (1996–2007)

1996 June	*NHT* of Australia Bill for a $1 billion trust fund to protect the environment, after sale of half of Telstra. The NHT concept came from Landcare, which started small in 1985.
1996 Sept	Second State of the Environment Report released.
1996	Great Australian Bight Marine Park declared.
1996	Australia bans the import and manufacture of ozone depleting chemicals.
1996	National Strategy for the Conservation of Australia's Biological Diversity.
1996	*IPA Program* established for Indigenous landowners to develop, declare and manage IPAs on their lands. The program attracted ~ $100m, over 1996-2013.
1997 Nov	Prime Minister's 5-year $180m *Safeguarding the Future,* to address climate change.
1997	Australia's Wetlands Policy announced.
1997 June	*EPBC* Bill passed through the Senate.
1997 Dec	Minister Hill secured agreement to an Australian emissions target, of an 8% increase over 1990 levels, at the 1997 international climate change negotiations.
1997	Prime Minister Howard refuses to ratify Kyoto Protocol.
1998	Nantawarrina, South Australia, the first IPA, is announced.
1998 Dec	Australia's Oceans Policy launched, to manage 14m sq. km of ocean.
1998 April	Australian Greenhouse Office established.

Table 1.2: Federal environment policy, key events 1992-2014 (cont.)

1998 Nov	Australia's National Greenhouse Strategy launched.
1999 Aug	National Packaging Covenant signed by Australian Government, New Zealand, Australian State governments, local governments and some industries.
1999 Nov	Measures for a Better Environment, $400 million over four years, negotiated with the Democrats to achieve Senate passage of the GST legislation.
2000 July	*Product Stewardship (Oil) Act 2000* comes into force.
2000 July	*EPBC Act 1999* comes into force.
2000 Nov	Greater Blue Mountains Area inscribed on World Heritage List.
2001	*Regional Forest Agreements* process completed.
2001 May	Announcement of a 5-year $1bn *NHT* extension, commencing in 2002–03.
2001 July	Environmental assessment process begins for Commonwealth fisheries, under *EPBC Act*.
2001 Sept	Australian Government, NSW, Victoria, SA, WA and ACT sign up to the 2001 National Biodiversity Conservation Strategy.
2002 Jan	*Fuel Quality Standards Act 2000* comes into effect.
2002 March	Third SoE report (for the five years to 2001) released.
2002 April	Envirofund ($20 million) launched as part of *NHT* to fund community grants.
2002 June	Prime Minister Howard announced Australia would not ratify the Kyoto Protocol.
2002 Oct	Heard Island and McDonald Islands Marine Reserve declared under *EPBC Act*.
2003 Sept	National Greenhouse Gas Inventory reports.
2003 Oct	15 'National Biodiversity Hotspots' announced.
2003 Nov	Living Murray Initiative of $500 million to restore flows to the river announced.

2003 Dec	Great Barrier Reef Water Quality Protection Plan finalised.
2004 Jan	New national heritage regime under *EPBC Act* came into effect, covering natural, Indigenous and historic heritage values.
2004 April	*State of the Air* report released, first comprehensive picture of Australia's air quality.
2004	Australia's first national energy policy announced: *Securing Australia's Energy Future.*
2004 June	National Water Initiative and National Water Commission agreed by COAG.
2004 July	GBR Marine Park new zoning plan increased the area of 'no take' fishing zones in the Park from 4.5% to 33.3%, supported by initial (up to) $86.7m for structural adjustment.
2005 May	Commonwealth Environment Research Facilities program announced, $100m over five years, in part to replace termination of environment-related Coop. Research Centres.
2006 May	Regional Marine Planning funding extended for four years, at $10m per annum.
2006 May	Tasmanian Community Forest Agreement announced.
2006 Dec	African bigheaded ant successfully eradicated from Kakadu by CSIRO and Parks Australia – claimed to be the largest pest-ant eradication in the world.
2007 Jan	National Plan for Water Security $10 billion over 10 years.
2007 May	*Working on Country* announced with $47.9 million over four years for 100 ranger jobs.
2007 May	Environmental Stewardship Program announced with $50 million over four years with follow-up payments for up to 15 years.
2007 May	A further $2 billion announced for the *NHT* and $1.4 billion for the National Action Plan for Salinity and Water Quality.
2007 May	$70.6 million over four years provided to administer the *EPBC Act 1999.*
2007 May	$200 million provided over six years for Community Water Grants.

ALP Rudd (Dec 2007–June 2010)

2007 Dec	Australia finally signed the 1997 Kyoto Protocol to limit international emissions.

Table 1.2: Federal environment policy, key events 1992-2014 (cont.)

2007 Dec	Rudd Government confirmed commitments made in the election process for $815 million for a *Solar Homes and Communities Plan*, $507 million for a *Solar Hot Water Program*, $361.6 million for a *National Solar Schools Plan.*
2008 May	$2.2 billion announced for the *Caring for Our Country* program over five years including an injection of $50 million over five years to 2012–13 for IPAs, a quadrupling of funds for the NRS, and $200 million Reef Rescue plan for the Great Barrier Reef.
2008 May	*Green Loans Program* ($300m over five years) announced, designed to provide up to 200,000 low-interest green loans of up to $10,000 over five years to install water, energy and solar efficient products in homes, and reduce national greenhouse gas emissions.
2009 Feb	Part of the $42 billion National Building and Jobs Plan, the $4.3b Energy Efficient Homes Package included the *Home Insulation Program*, to insulate 2.9m homes to help households save up to 40% on their electricity bills (Prime Minister, 3 February 2009a).
2009 May	Additional $33m to manage national parks (Kakadu, Uluru, Kata Tjuta etc.) and to support the National Landscapes program (Tourism Australia/Parks Australia partnership).

ALP Gillard (June 2010-June 2013)

2011 May	Release of Australia's first national strategy on population. It provided funding, nominally for 'sustainable population', but in effect mainly for suburban jobs, regional development.
2011 May	$84.2 million over four years to continue the Environmental Stewardship Program.
2011 May	$9.7 million for management of proposed marine reserves and bioregional plans.
2011 Dec	$946 million Biodiversity Fund over six years announced, in negotiations between the Gillard Government and Australian Greens, to get carbon tax legislation through.
2012 May	Continuation of *Caring for Our Country*, with $2.2 billion over 2013–2018.

ALP Rudd (27 June 2013–September 2013)

2012 Nov	Proclamation of more than 2.3m sq. km. within the network of Commonwealth marine reserves for protection under the *EPBC Act*.
2013 July	*Caring for Our Country* to be delivered through separate streams – sustainable environment and sustainable farming – ending the long-standing joint management arrangements between the Federal Environment and Agriculture Departments.

LPA Abbott (From 18 September 2013)	
2013 Oct	Government announced framework to streamline environmental approvals including through bilateral agreements with States to secure 'swifter' decisions.
2013 Dec	Government announced replacing *Caring for Our Country* with a National Landcare Program. The Biodiversity Fund was wound up, and its uncommitted funding reallocated.
2013 Dec	Royal Commission into *Home Insulation Program* established, with the Environment Department contributing $6.9 million from uncommitted *Caring for Our Country* funds.
2013 Dec	Release of Emissions Reduction Fund Green Paper as centrepiece of the Government's Direct Action Plan – their replacement policy to the carbon tax.
2014 Feb	Legislation to establish a 'Green Army' introduced, to support local environment conservation projects, with a target of 15,000 participants by 2018.
2014 Mar	Abbott Government confirmed its commitment to removing the Carbon Tax.
2014 Apr	Macquarie Island declared pest free (funded under *Caring for Our Country*).

Sources: Environment Portfolio Budget, Annual Reports, Environment Budget Overview/Statement booklets produced by the Environment Department from 2000–01 through to 2008–09 (Australian Government, 1996-2013) (Department of Environment, 2013b), http://www.environment.gov.au/about/publications/budget/2013/pubs/pbs-portfolio-budget-statements-2013–14.pdf, Appendix B, internal 'History of the Department of Environment and Heritage' (2004), http://www.environment.gov.au/minister/archive/index.html other docs (Accessed Aug 2012), http://www.environment.gov.au/minister/hunt/2014/index.html (Accessed Apr 2014).

As these reversals indicate, the federal role in environmental policy is not necessarily a one-way street. Indeed, in some respects, the Environment Department's positive first thirty years over 1971-2001 are beginning to resemble a *trente glorieuses*.

Nevertheless, the point remains that federal environment policy has been much enlarged in its reach and sophistication. It has had distinct successes. Even though it may appear to go into reverse at times, it seems unlikely to revert to its weak and poorly articulated pre-1971 self.

Environment Ministers begin to flex their muscles

The federal Environment Ministers appointed from 1988 through to 2013 are shown at Table 1.3. Senator Richardson only had a two-year (1988-1990) initial stint as Environment Minister. But he and the very different Senator Hill (Minister from 1996-2001) were the two ministers most often mentioned by interviewees for this book as having the capacity to engineer the best results from the policy mandate.

Table 1.3: List of Federal Environment Ministers, 1988–2014

Year	Environment Minister	Federal Party
Appointed Sep 2013	The Hon Greg Hunt MP	Liberal
Sep 2010 – Sept 2013	The Hon Tony Burke AM MP	Labor
Dec 2007 – Sept 2010	The Hon Peter Garrett AM MP	Labor
Jan 2007 – Dec 2007	The Hon Malcolm Turnbull MP	Liberal
July 2004 – Jan 2007	Senator the Hon Ian Campbell MP	Liberal
Nov 2001 – July 2004	The Hon Dr David Kemp MP	Liberal
Mar 1996 – Nov 2001	Senator the Hon Robert Hill MP	Liberal
Mar 1994 – Mar 1996	Senator the Hon John Faulkner MP	Labor
Mar 1994 – Mar 1994	The Hon G Richardson MP	Labor
Apr 1990 – Mar 1994	The Hon Ros Kelly MP	Labor
Jan 1988 – Apr 1990	Senator the Hon G Richardson MP	Labor

Source: http://www.environment.gov.au/node/13269 (Accessed April 2014)

The tactical efforts of Senator Richardson to achieve the Wet Tropics World Heritage are of note. On his watch, Table 1.1 also has the announcement of a Decade of Landcare, the One Billion trees, and the ban on chlorofluorocarbons. The table then shows a lull in key environmental events, between 1993 and 1996.

1996 ushered in the Howard Government and its capable Environment Minister, Senator Robert Hill. His tenure, and related changes to legislative and administrative arrangements, strengthened the hand of the Government in environment policy.

As the Leader of the Senate, Hill was a key Cabinet member. For the first time, the Government (notably Liberal and not Labor) had an Environment Minister in Cabinet. Hill quickly won Cabinet applause, by brokering for Australia an emissions 'reduction' target actually enabling a generous increase in Australia's greenhouse gas emissions (Table 1.2) over 1990-2012.

Under the guidance of Minister Hill and his Departmental Secretary, Roger Beale, the Environment Portfolio grew from a minor and fragmented player into a recognisable force in Cabinet. Coming from a 'central agency' (that is, Prime Minister and Cabinet, Finance, or Treasury) Beale understood the importance of orderly governance as a precondition for effective policy development. Up until his time, the Department had been more in the nature of five 'fiefdoms' (national parks, heritage, policy, environment protection, and Antarctic Division). These often competed against one another, thus failing to present a united working front to government. The five agencies were now merged into a coherent Environment Department.

The combined efforts of Hill as Minister, and Beale as Secretary of a united Department, opened the way to reform a plethora of disjointed environment laws. These laws had been largely unchanged for 25 years. They focused on Commonwealth intervention, often 'by exception', or at the last minute. By the end of the 1990s, a new *EPBC Act* was in place. As noted above, it enshrined the Environment Minister as the decision-maker on matters of NES.

Minor parties begin to exert their influence on environmental policy

In Tables 1.1 and 1.2 there is also a story of minor rising party influence. While this influence has tended to be opportunistic and inconsistent, nevertheless it has been a significant element in the long-term trajectory of federal environment policy.

Early on, environmental groups had played key roles in the milestone decisions to protect Fraser Island and the Gordon River. As Environment Minister, but with a reputation as a political dealmaker, Senator Richardson was well attuned to the importance of the Green vote in certain electorates. This was a motivating factor in his 1988 push for the Wet Tropics World Heritage listing.

In 1999, the Democrats extracted a discrete $400 million Better Environment deal from the Liberals, as a trade-off for its GST legislation. In similar vein, the near $1 billion Biodiversity Fund of 2011 was a trade-off with the Greens for the passage of Labor's carbon tax legislation.

1.3 Federal environment policies of 1993–2013

The research for this book focuses on the 1993-2013 period. It considers the broad range of federal environment policies and programs that were in evidence over that period. Within that, it homes in on 12 particular policies and programs selected for their size or significance.

The early 1990s were chosen as a satisfactory starting point. By that time, a certain level of breadth and maturity had been reached with the environmental policy apparatus in federal government and in its bureaucracy.

Broadly speaking, the three tiers of government had agreed their respective roles and responsibilities in environment policy. New international philosophies for a more integrated approach to environment protection had filtered through to the Australia policy scene, including the 'central' federal agencies of Prime Minister and Cabinet, Finance, and Treasury. The federal Environment Department itself had begun to operate more as a unified policy entity, rather than a loose set of competing agencies.

Regular State of the Environment Reports, an increasing mass of scientific studies, and better Departmental databases, offered a better information base from which to build credible federal policies. Cabinet was beginning to consider or agree on national environment strategies. A more diverse suite of national environment policies and programs was beginning to evolve, with serious levels of funding commitment.

Over the study period, the Department implemented a wide range of national strategies, legislation, and funded programs. To situate the 12 policies chosen for detailed study, this full suite of policies is summarised below.

Environment Department policies over 1993-2013

In the wake of the 1992 National Strategy for Environmentally Sustainable Development (NSESD), federal government has issued national environment strategies on matters such forests, biodiversity, climate change, oceans policy, and population policy. These are summarised at Table 1.4.

These strategies were useful to the extent that they established frameworks for new policy measures, encouraged consideration of sustainability criteria, and improved consultation and data collation. They provided a mechanism for greater transparency in federal-state environment collaboration on environmental matters.

Though environmental gains through this consensus approach ultimately were disappointing, the national strategies reflected a maturing of the governance arrangements for environment protection in Australia, at least up until September 2013.

Typically, the national strategies articulated policy intentions, characterised by aspirational aims, yet with little by way of measurable targets within specified timeframes. They were bedevilled by a lack of political will, vague or unrealistic targets, and inadequate funding. In Marsh and McConnell's Framework (2010) terms, they were successful on process and political dimensions but not the programmatic dimension.

Table 1.4: National Environment Strategies, 1992–2011

Date of release	Strategy
1992	The National Strategy for Ecologically Sustainable Development (NSESD)
1992	National Forest Policy Statement
1992	National Greenhouse Response Strategy
1995	Regional Forest Agreement (RFA) Process
1996 to 2010	National Strategies for the Conservation of Australia's Biological Diversity
1999	National Oceans Policy
1999	Strategic Plan of Action for the National Representative System of Marine Protected Areas
2011	National Population Strategy

As discussed above, the most important piece of federal environment legislation enacted within the 1993-2013 study period was the *EPBC Act 1999*. The Department administers numerous other Acts ranging widely over aspects of the environment, from sea dumping to the *Product Stewardship Act 2011*. The Natural Heritage Trust (NHT) has a legislative base in the *Natural Heritage Trust of Australia Act 1997*.

Following the positive impact of the *Ozone Protection and Synthetic Greenhouse Gas Management Act 1989*, the *Fuel Quality Standards Act 2000* is also recognised as successful. Both Acts had bipartisan support and an effective process for implementation. Their objectives continue to be met and they have both delivered significant environmental benefits.

The funded programs delivered by the Department over 1993-2013 may be grouped into the following categories:

*   Biodiversity protection – including Landcare, NHT, Caring for Our Country and the Biodiversity Fund

*   Climate change and energy efficiency programs – including renewable energy programs, greenhouse gas abatement programs, Solar Rebate Programs, Smart Grid, Solar Cities, the Home Insulation Program and the Green Loans Program

*   Water reform policies and programs – water quality, Murray Darling Basin, infrastructure investment, structural adjustment

- Coastal, oceans and marine programs including Coasts and Clean Seas, Coastcare, Reef Rescue, and Marine Protected Areas

- Indigenous land management programs – Contract Employment Program for Aboriginals in Natural and Cultural Resource Management (CEPANCRM), Indigenous Protected Areas, Working on Country

- Protected area management – national parks and the National Reserve System

- Pollution control programs to address air quality, chemical and waste management.

Environment Department policies chosen for particular attention

Within the overall suite of Departmental strategies, legislation, and funded programs, the research undertaken for this book sought to give particular attention to a smaller set of significant policies. Climate change policy, for one, was set aside. With its extreme political turbulence and sensitivity, even a capacity to derail federal governments or federal party leaders, it is worthy of extensive study in its own right, and has indeed attracted such. Also, for part of the study period, 2007-2013, climate change policy was not in the federal Environment Department.

Six biodiversity policies and programs, and six energy or solar policies and programs, were selected for closer attention, and these are displayed in Table 1.5.

These 12 policies or programs were targeted because of their environmental impact, funding levels, and geographic scale. Eight of them were important national programs that took up large chunks of the Department's annual program (grant) expenditure during their years of operation. Unless terminated early, these programs ran for at least one forward-estimates period of four years, and some of them continued after 2013.

The other four policies in Table 1.5, the EPBC Act, Fuel Quality Standards Act, Regional Forest Agreements, and Marine Protected Areas, are diverse 'lighthouse' policies that have been significant to the Department over a number of years.

Table 1.5: Twelve federal environment programs or policies given particular attention [1]

Biodiversity programs and policies	Energy efficiency and solar programs and policies
The Natural Heritage Trust (NHT) ($3bn budget over 1996-2008) [2]	Home Insulation Program ($2.7bn over 2009-2011)
Caring for Our Country ($2.25bn over 2008-2013)	Solar Homes and Communities Plan ($815m over 2006-2010)
Working on Country ($298m over 2007-2013)	Solar Hot Water Rebate Program ($507m over 2008-2012)
EPBC Act 1999	National Solar Schools Program ($362m over 2008-2012)
The Regional Forest Agreements (RFA)	Green Loans Program ($300m over 2008-2013)
Marine Protected Areas (MPAs)	Fuel Quality Standards Act 2000

Sources: Environment Department Annual Reports 1993-94 to 2012-13 Australian Government. 1996-2013; *Past Budgets* [Online]. Available: http://www.budget.gov.au/past_budgets.htm [Accessed 19 March 2014]; Department of Environment. 2013b. *Annual Reports* [Online]. Available: http://www.environment.gov.au/topics/about-us/accountability-reporting/annual-reports [Accessed 29 October 2013].; Department of Environment Budgets Australian Government. 1996-2013. *Past Budgets* [Online]. Available: http://www.budget.gov.au/past_budgets.htm [Accessed 19 March 2014]; Commonwealth Environment Budget Expenditure 2000-01 to 2003-04, Environment Budget Statement 2004-05.

(1) Chapter 5 case studies Working on Country, Home Insulation and Fuel Quality, also an additional and contrasting policy, the Sustainable Population Strategy.

(2) Some programs were terminated early, and not all allocated budgets were expensed.

Chapter 2

Ideas of Policy Success and Failure

This chapter works through the theories and concepts relating to policy success and failure. This literature helped to shape the interview questions and the assessment of the policies and programs that interviewees for this book raised and discussed.

Section 2.1 proposes a working definition of policy, applicable to environment policy. We found limited guidance for the interviews in the literature on policy implementation (Section 2.2) or in the common 'checklists' for policy success (Section 2.3). Section 2.4 canvasses some key theories about key factors for policy success. While this uncovers no single overarching theory that can be applied readily to environment policy, it discovers useful organising principles for the interviews, and for the questions that could be posed.

The final section introduces the Marsh and McConnell Framework, which assesses program success or failure along process, programmatic and political dimensions. Among the recent research, this Framework appears to be the best tool to structure the environment policy case studies and cross-validate the interviewee ratings of program success and failure.

2.1 The public policy context

Why do some environment policies succeed when others fail? Political economic, economic, and environment, theories offer various underlying explanations.

Political economy considers how political considerations are influencing the policy choices (Howlett et al., 2009, Walker, 1994). Economic explanations of environment policy failure focus on the failure of the market to factor waste, scarcity and intrinsic 'values' into the price of natural assets. Typically, environment theory explanations of why environment policy fails reside in the dominance of economy over ecology.

Despite their extensive theorising, the political scientists, economists and environmental theorists have done little to ensure policy success in environment policy. Policy officials face the task of designing and implementing workable policy with no definitive theoretical guidance.

As we are looking at success or failure from the perspective of the policy official, public policy theory appears to be the best body of underpinning theoretical knowledge. As we are working in the Australian policy context, our attention falls on the Australian literature. We also adduce UK, North American and European literature about policymaking, in relation to democracies and Westminster-style governments.

There is a distinction in the theoretical literature between the 'positivist' interest in what policy is and how policy is done, and the 'normative' interest in how policy should be done to deliver better outcomes.

Colebatch et al.'s (2010, 16) *Working for Policy,* by their own assessment, is positivist. It focuses on what policy workers do, rather than assessing the outcome of their work. On the other hand, Weimer and Vining (2005), Barrett and Fudge (1981) and Pülzl and Treib (2007, 90) are examples of the normative approach that we lean towards. Our main driver was why environment policies succeed or fail on the ground, rather than a detached theoretical interest in the policy process as such.

Colebatch (1998, 3, 111, 2007, 1, 6) has observed that practitioners and academics describe the policy-making experience differently. This suggests that practitioners will find limited guidance in the theoretical literature, on how to secure policy success. After years scrutinising public policy theories for clues to assist practitioners in implementing policy that works, a noted US professor of public administration concluded "theories about policy implementation have been almost embarrassingly plentiful, yet theoretical consensus is not on the horizon." (O'Toole, 2004, 310).

"The number of variables offered by researchers as plausible parts of the explanation for implementation results is large and growing," O'Toole continued. "Disputes among proponents of different perspectives on the implementation question have filled volumes. Different investigators pursue explanations for different kinds of dependent variables, with relatively little dialogue regarding what might be the most appropriate *explanandum.* After hundreds of empirical studies, validated findings are relatively scarce. Few long-term longitudinal studies have been completed. And, most telling of all, those who have specialised in studying implementation questions systematically have had relatively little to say to practitioners."

Given this disconnect in the literature between theory and practice, and the inherent complexity of policymaking, this research project did not fit easily into any one theoretical framework for public policy. It gave up searching for any single framework that offered the most explanatory power.

Rather, we draw insights from the broad church of policy theories. Consistent with Nowlin (2011), Moran et al. (2008), Winter (2007) and Yanow (1996), that means referring to the broad accumulation of pertinent knowledge in public policy theory.

At the outset, there is the problem that policy theorists have had no settled or common definition of public policy. Diverse approaches are represented in the works of Hogwood and Gunn (1984), Parsons (1995), Thomas (2007), Dye (2008), Kraft and Furlong (2010, 5) and Maddison and Denniss (2009, 3-4).

Dye's simple definition of public policy (Dye, 2008) is "whatever a government chooses to do or not to do". Dovers' (2005, 18) broader definition of public policy in the Australian context is the "processes and decisions enabled, made and/or communicated by government and other institutions operating in the public domain".

Figure 2.1: Working definition of public policy in the Australian context

> The decisions government takes through formal processes such as Cabinet, to implement a course of action to improve outcomes for the good of the public, or to respond to a specific interest, group or political imperative.

The working definition of public policy at Figure 2.1 applies to this book. It is synthesised from definitions in the public policy literature, as adapted for the Australian context. It is readily applicable to environment policy. It was the starting point for this exploration of how the officials predict and pursue policy success.

This working definition requires that a policy 'decision' be formalised in some way. It recognises that, when faced with a policy problem, policymakers lean towards action. It plays down matters of redistribution and equity – but Chapter 6 comes back to these. It avoids the question of whose perspective is best suited to assess the 'good' of the public. It embodies the notion of change for the better, without defining 'better'.

The definition is based on our years of policy experience. We intuit that practitioners understand public policy as the decisions taken by government to implement a course of action to improve specific outcomes, for the good of the public, or as a pragmatic response to a powerful vested interest with political sway.

In Chapter 3, a paradoxical finding will emerge. Much like the literature, the interviewees struggle to define precisely or consistently what government 'policy' means. Nevertheless, they intuitively recognise those of their colleagues who are 'good' at it. They also claim to have an intuitive advance sense of whether or not policies are going to work out successfully.

2.2 Theorising about policy implementation

Reviewing the public policy literature, we found few articles relating policy implementation to policy success. Policy theory has offered practitioners no predictive tools for policy success (O'Toole, 2004) and little practical advice on how to anticipate and avoid implementation problems (Weimer and Vining, 2005).

Weimer and Vining first published their policy analysis book as long ago as 1989. Their big question was "What factors influence the likelihood of successful implementation?"

To fill the gap in advice for policy practitioners, they offered the concept of scenario writing. They suggested that policy analysts 'forward map' how their chosen policy, and other alternative approaches, might unfold in practice. They recognised that 'forward mappers' had to be courageous in prediction. This called for "dirty mindedness", thinking about what could go wrong and who might have an incentive to make it go wrong (Weimer and Vining, 2005, 280-281). Since they did their work, related strategies have evolved, such as risk assessment, gaming analysis and scenario planning. These are applied widely in public policy and in business.

After 30 years of research, O'Toole (2004, 309) wryly observed that, if theoretical knowledge was going to have practical application in *any* subject, policy implementation ought to be a frontrunner. He concluded that practitioners couldn't apply theories of policy implementation to diagnose policy dilemmas and calibrate their responses. He explained this in terms of the fragmented and disputed theory and the complexity of policy. As he saw it, managers of public programs typically face a "nonlinear reality" with complicated interactions that are difficult to model or predict.

Though implementation theory falls short as a predictive tool, O'Toole still thought that practitioners could ask 'What do I need to pay attention to?' to improve the likelihood of success. In his shortlist, he thought they should analyse the channels of influence that were most likely to shape the actions of other involved parties; consider actions and possibilities from multiple perspectives; and sort through points of leverage to identify options and trade-offs. Also, they should think through how the objectives, the information, and the degree of control held by policy actors, can combine to affect the implementation process and can interact with external circumstances.

O'Toole began to bridge the disconnection between the theory and practice of policymaking. His work was instructive, because he thought about how the motivation, gaming and leverage of policy players, including policy officials, interacted with external factors to condition policy outcomes.

More recently, McConnell (2010b) has touched on the question of predicting policy outcomes. Although it may not be possible to predict policy success, he thought, at least one can be aware that some policies are riskier than others. "We cannot predict the future," he concluded, "but we can at least use our intuition to map out one or more plausible scenarios of whether policy options might succeed or fail."

Summing up, the recent literature on policy implementation is quite small, and it did not provide much guidance for this research. However, the perspicacity of Weimer and Vining, O'Toole, and McConnell stands out. Their extensive research keeps coming back to the idea of policy officials having a certain capacity to apply informed judgments in their pursuit of successful policy outcomes. This research, particularly in its discussion of the 'agency' of policy officials, vindicates their approaches.

2.3 Theories of preconditions for policy success

Although the 'policy implementation' approach is limited, there is a broader literature positing 'preconditions' for policy success, or 'factors' associated with policy success. To guide the interviews with the policy officials, this work was studied in some detail.

The intuitively appealing idea of certain logical steps or checklists as preconditions to policy success is important in the theory, and also common in practice guides for policy officials.

As early as 1979, Sabatier and Mazmanian (1979, 489-492) developed a 'six-step' model for policy implementation. Their steps covered policy objectives, validity of the causal theory, implementation process, commitment of officials, support from legislature and interest groups, and no socioeconomic detriment. Hogwood and Gunn's (1984) list for success had ten slightly different preconditions to the Sabatier list. They wanted one 'obedient' agency to be responsible for implementation. The American, Bardach (2009, xvii, xvi, 145), pitched his pathway to effective policy in terms of eight simple imperatives. These were to define the problem, assemble evidence, construct the alternatives, select the criteria, project the outcomes, confront the trade-offs, decide, and tell the story.

Work in the 1990s by the UK Cabinet Office and National Audit Office (Bullock et al., 1999, Great Britain Cabinet Office, 1999a, b) informed contemporary UK and Australian checklists of good practice for government policy officials.

Althaus et al. (2007, 166-167) reviewed the UK literature, to set out theory, design, and implementation pre-conditions for successful policy implementation. Influenced by Althaus, Australia's own National Audit Office (ANAO) put out a *Better Practice Guide* (ANAO, 2006) with seven high-level questions for policy implementers. While the ANAO kit emphasised options, risks, leadership, timeframes, resources, and stakeholders, still it begged the question of what the "critical implementation success factors" were.

Concerned by federal "policy by fiat" or "policy on the run", and rattled by the Home Insulation Program failure, the Institute of Public Administration, Australia (IPAA, April 2012) issued ten criteria for a sound business case for new policies. The IPAA criteria pick up items such as demonstrable need, clear objectives, considering all the policy options, and communications strategy. The IPAA checklist introduces the notion of feedback to refine the policy design, and captures the importance of selling the policy to the public.

These practitioner documents as developed in UK and Australia do provide some useful guidance on how to avoid failure and achieve success. They help to bridge the gap between policy theory and practice. However, official government policy-advice documents typically give little consideration to the underlying *political* drivers, the impact of political influences on how a policy unfolds, or the implications of underlying political forces on whether the policy was a success or not.

In summary, the literature on 'preconditions' for success is a useful starting point for identifying 'common sense' requirements for policy success. Strong themes in this literature are the critical importance of setting clear objectives, and attending to the interests of those impacted by a policy. Such themes guided the structure of the interviews.

2.4 Theories of factors driving policy success

To further inform the research and the interview questions, there was also a sifting through the literature on what might be termed the 'drivers' of policy success. Policy theory and practice have evolved, from the 1950s rationalist attempts to explain the 'science' of policy, through to more recent governance and complexity theories. One constant in this evolution of theory and practice is the focus on what works in policymaking. Table 2.1 sets out the dominant theories and concepts relevant to this study over three timeframes, along with the parallel concepts in public administration.

Table 2.1: Fashions in policy theory and public administration, 1950s to date

Era	Policy theories	Policy administration
1950s to late 1970s	Policy science Policy cycle approach Rational choice theory	Grounded in science and economics Tools include cost-benefit analysis, rational hierarchical planning
Late 1970s to late 1990s	Agenda-setting theory Design theory Implementation theories – top down and bottom up NPM Evidence-based policymaking	Concerned with how issues arose and fell away from a government's policy agenda Identified design as a key stage Grounded in models of better management to improve efficiency and performance Cast policy as rational rather than political
Late 1990s to present	Advocacy Coalition Theory Governance Theory Complexity Theory Complex Adaptive Systems Political risk Policy success	Incorporated a broader notion of government Grounded in concepts of complexity, partnerships, networks, collaboration Invoked notions of whole-of-government, joined-up government Focused on accountability, contracting out and contestability of advice to government Greater attention to policy communication strategies and the role of the media Construes policy as a 'wicked problem'

Key source: Pollitt and Bouchaert (2011)

One problem is that 'policy success' is a fairly recent theoretical construct in the literature. The concept of success, rather than being a unified theme, surfaces under different guises at different times in various branches of the literature. The 'policy cycle' (Laswell, 1956) was used as the organising principle in the literature search. Sabatier (2007) and others have criticised this idealised concept. Still, it is a useful way to organise the messy threads of policy development. Also, it resonates with policy practitioners.

Figure 2.2: The policy cycle

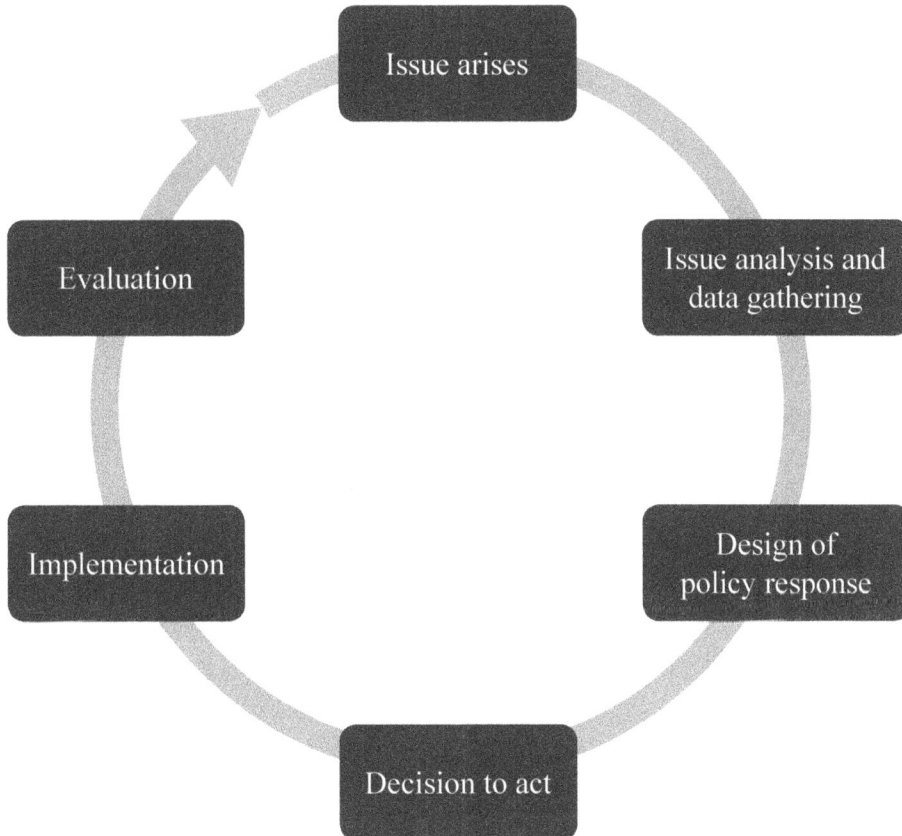

Sources: Adapted from the many variations found in the literature (Althaus et al., 2007, Davis et al., 1993, Edwards, 2001, Howlett et al., 2009, Kraft and Furlong, 2010, Moran et al., 2008, Parsons, 1995).

Accordingly, the factors for policy success are discussed in a similar order to the key stages of the idealised policy cycle as depicted at Figure 2.2. This same order also proved useful for structuring the interview questions.

Policy origins: theories of agenda setting

To what extent do the 'origins' of a policy have implications for its chance of success? Not that much, the literature suggests.

Policy ideas may emerge from a few crucial actors or events. Usually, the origins are diffuse. Baumgartner and Jones (2009) refer to the difficulty of isolating policy origins as the 'Silent Spring' phenomenon. Rachael Carson's (1962) *Silent Spring* warning on toxic chemicals followed concerns expressed by others, but she gets the main credit for the policy idea.

Rather than policy origins as such, Kingdon (2011) focused on policy 'windows'. Drawing on his original 1984 work on agenda setting, he argued that success was more likely when a policy 'window' of favourable political forces conjoined the problem stream with the stream of available solutions. He was an early theorist to play up the role of "policy entrepreneurs" both inside and outside government. He referred to the "messiness, accident" of policy formation. He thought entrepreneurs ought to stand ready to seize scarce and unpredictable policy openings. A number of the interviewees simulated that kind of policy opportunism.

Another American scholar, Downs (1972), concluded early on that the rise and fall of environment issues didn't really correlate with the intrinsic importance of the issues. Similarly, Dovers (2013) found no inherent pattern or party-political logic in what had grabbed the Australian Government's environment policy attention over the previous 50 years. Issues might variously be driven by international commitments, the appeal of iconic places, short-term electoral advantage, or sudden ecological crises.

Nevertheless, the history of federal environment policy in Australia (Department of Environment and Heritage, 2004) suggests some value in examining the significance of policy origins for policy success. In response, the interviewees were asked, "Do you know where the policy came from – how it got on the Government's agenda?"

Policy design and implementation

A 1980s wave of policy theorists thought that policy would succeed if design and implementation got the right attention (Linder and Peters, 1987, 459). Mayntz (1983, 124) observed that perfect implementation cannot ensure policy success if the program adopts the wrong design. Theorists like Dryzek (1987), Schneider and Ingram (1988) and Weimer and Vining (2005) continued Mayntz's quest for a design-led solution to policy success.

Schneider and Sidney (2009, 9-11) tried to reignite the focus on policy design, which they said ought to be incorporated explicitly in theories of the policy process. Policy design theory, they said, pushes scholars to think about the "feed-forward" effects of policy, allowing outcomes to be linked back to original policymaking processes in which compromise and rhetoric are imposed on the original design.

Overall, the policy design literature seems not to have left behind a robust theory, framework or model for predicting policy success.

This book takes 'implementation' of policy to cover both the delivery process and the outcome – whether the stated objective was achieved. Pressman and Wildavsky's (1973) work is a pioneering study in policy implementation, showing the gap between political claims of policy success and the reality of implementation. They showed how a federal (Washington) program to create employment for unemployed inner city residents foundered on the other side of the country in Oakland, California, with only about 10 per cent of its budget spent. Later, Wildavsky (1979, 17) came to see that solving public policy in the American context involved compromises between resources and objectives, planning and politics, scepticism and dogma. He recognised that assessing policy success or failure involved judgment rather than scientific precision.

Following up Pressman and Wildavsky, other theorists scrutinised implementation as a way to explain success or failure of a policy intervention. The 1980s saw 'top-down' and 'bottom-up' perspectives (Pülzl and Treib, 2007, 89). Mazmanian and Sabatier (1983) theorised that policy decisions, if delivered through a hierarchical and well-structured implementation process with the right controls, resources and incentives, had more scope for successful implementation. Conversely, Lipsky (1980) gave primacy to the role of "street-level bureaucrats". His notion of instrumental bureaucrats implementing, and to some degree defining, public policy becomes important for analysing the interviews.

In the policy literature, it is not easy to separate design from implementation. Nevertheless, on our reading, these types of questions probe critical elements of the design phase:

- Is close attention paid to alternative options to address the problem?

- Are the proposed tools suited to the issue and likely to deliver the outcome?

- Have unintended consequences been thought through?

Similarly, these types of questions probe critical practical issues in the implementation phase:

- Is there a well-developed implementation or project management plan?

- Have risks been identified and management strategies put in place?

- Does the team charged with implementation have the right skill sets?

- Are there clear governance structures, with adequate budgets and timeframes?

- Are the Government and Executive committed to a successful delivery?

Taking up such questions, the policy officials interviewed were tested on policy designs, and whether or not these included consideration of alternative policy instruments.

'New Public Management' and evidence-based policymaking

So-called 'New Public Management' (NPM) and 'evidence-based policymaking' (EBPM) are two later phases of implementation studies that also influenced the present research.

Barrett (2004) perceived the 20 years of NPM up to 2000 as a new phase in implementation studies. Its advocates, she suggested, believed that NPM's focus on accountability, contracting out and performance frameworks had addressed key problems in implementation failure. Performance measures and performance contracts, so it was claimed, would address what it was that was to be delivered by policy. Privatisation, marketisation and public/private partnerships would address resource issues, supposedly reducing public costs and injecting private sector funds. Accountability measures and contracting out would bring the implementation agencies to heel. The mantra was "Let the managers manage".

Policy academics never really stopped doing implementation studies, so Barrett contended, they just adopted the language of NPM. Although NPM brought rigour and theoretical discipline to the practice of policy, its benefits now seem debatable.

The more recent NPM literature promotes EBPM as a key to policy success. It says a policy based on evidence is more likely to succeed than one that is not. 'Evidence' is imputed to be neutral and objective and therefore essential (Banks, 2009, Howlett, 2009, Nutley, 2003, Nutley et al., 2009, Smith, 2009). In the Canadian context, Howlett et al. (2009) saw EBPM as an effort to shore up rationality in the policy process, by prioritising data-based decision-making criteria over less formal, and more intuitive, policymaking.

Other writers countered that 'evidence' is subjective and open to misuse, seeing ideological tones in the push for EBPM (Boaz and Pawson, 2005, Freiberg and Carson, 2010, Greenhalgh and Russell, 2009, Head, 2008, Marsten and Watts, 2003). Parsons (2002) critically reviewed EBPM, particularly as formulated by the Blair Labour Government in British Cabinet and Audit Office papers of 1999-2001. "What matters is what works" became a Blair policy mantra, supposedly to trump ideologically based decision-making with evidence-based decision-making. But Parsons saw this as a "muddled" form of managerialism at best. He reinterpreted the so-called "evidence-based" policy of the British Cabinet Office as "evidence controlled, managed and legitimated" policy.

Nevertheless, governments in the US, Canada, New Zealand, and Australia, began to adopt EBPM approaches (Nutley et al., 2009, 4). Australian Government guides and policy documents replayed the calls in the literature to substantiate policy proposals with evidence. However, there is now some disquiet that focus-group views have assumed the status of 'evidence' in Australian policymaking. These popular views have been one influence on the major policy flip-flops since the early 2000s on climate change.

Acknowledging the EBPM literature, when the interviewees elected to discuss particular policy processes in detail, they were asked directly about the role that evidence played.

More recent theories of success: governance and risk

A challenge in studying the policymaking process is that government itself is evolving. The 'governance' perspective brings into play notions of blurred responsibility and accountability, unintended consequences and governance failure (Stoker, 1998, 19). In the way that they construe policy success, governance models suggest a reduced role for central government and more decisive roles for public administrators negotiating with multiple actors and interest groups (Pülzl and Treib, 2007).

In Australian federal environment policy, the 1992 Ecologically Sustainable Development (ESD) process indicated a shift from 'government' to 'governance'. A wave of ESD taskforces combined the three levels of government with industry, non-government organisations (NGOs), subject-matter experts, and the community. The 2011 Tasmanian Forest Agreement between the forestry industry and conservationists is a more recent attempt at a similar approach. The external policy movers bypassed federal and State government, initially at least, in the formulation of this policy agreement.

Finally, an understanding of how politicians continually calculate the political risk of a policy action is a key ingredient to understanding public policymaking and why certain policy directions are pursued and others ignored (Althaus, 2008, 34). Althaus gave the example of British Prime Minister John Major paying dearly for his failure to reframe the 1997 mad cow disease crisis as a political survival issue rather than a scientific policy issue. Her interviews and case studies led her to the view that policy success, at least from a political risk perspective, depends on how well policymakers factor five themes into the policy design. These are policy and political uncertainty, the judgment of a champion politician, concerns for constituent and community impacts, awareness of attempts to control policy levers to meet political objectives, and reliance on the politics of a problem and not its policy technicalities. Althaus's concern with how policymakers construe political risk parallels the focus in this study on how policy officials construe policy success.

Table 2.2: Key factors for policy success as derived from the policy literature

Elements of policymaking	Questions likely to inform an understanding of policy success
Origins	What is the policy context?
	How did the policy come to be on the Government's policy and political agenda?
	Does the policy have the support of the Government and the administration?
	Did the policy proposal emerge from a broad base of community concern?
	Was it a response to a particular vested interest?
	Was it a response to a crisis?
Objectives	Is there a clear understanding of the problem to be addressed?
	Is there a causal link between the problem and the solution?
	Are the objectives clear and agreed?
	If there are multiple objectives, are they consistent or contradictory?
	Are the objectives achievable?
Design	Is close attention paid to alternative options to address the problem?
	Are the proposed tools suited to the issue and likely to deliver the outcome?
	Have unintended consequences been thought through?
Stakeholders	Is there sufficient community acceptance that there is a problem to be addressed?
	Has the policy development been informed by the knowledge and advice of stakeholders?
	Have all the interested and affected parties been identified?
	Are their positions well understood?
	Are there strategies in place to respond to specific interests affected by the policy?
Evidence	Is there sufficient evidence to support the need for intervention?
	Is there sufficient evidence to support the case for the solution proposed?
	Is there a method for capturing evidence to show the policy made a difference?
	Is any of the evidence highly contested or incomplete?

Elements of policymaking	Questions likely to inform an understanding of policy success
Implementation	Is there a well-developed implementation or project management plan?
	Have risks been identified and management strategies put in place?
	Does the team charged with implementation have the right skill sets?
	Are there clear governance structures in place setting out accountabilities?
	Are the budget and timeframe adequate?
	Are the Government and Executive committed to a successful delivery?
Communication	Is there a clear, simple narrative for the policy?
	Is there an active and positive media plan?
	Is there a communication plan to handle negative media reports?

The insights from the literature of this section are summarised in Table 2.2. This presents the key factors for success in an order that roughly aligns with the stages of the policy cycle at Figure 2.2. That does not imply a priority order, either in the literature, or for this study. It just means that the factors in Table 2.2 were used as a basis for selecting the interview questions, which appear in full in the Appendix. To recap, the question topics were broadly similar to the stages of the policy cycle at Figure 2.2, and the questions were posed in the same order.

2.5 Measuring policy success or failure

Along with interviewees' views on the *predictors* of environment policy success or failure, the author was just as interested in their assessments of success or failure of *existing* environmental policies.

In the classical depiction of the policy cycle, the 'evaluation' of the policy is the final stage that takes us full circle. Despite the tradition of policy evaluation and audit by government, Dye (2008) concluded that governments rarely examine seriously whether or not their policy choices have made much difference. In part, he took this view because he particularly wanted to know whether a policy had had a long-range beneficial effect on society. But evaluations and performance audits are potentially valuable tools to establish what worked. They can look back at whether public funds were used wisely and stated results achieved.

Marsh and McConnell (2010, 565-566) recognised the weakness of policy evaluation as a tool to determine policy success, in part because evaluations are often commissioned or conducted by government. Howlett et al. (2009, 183) thought that, often, policy evaluations aimed to provide just enough information to enable defensible claims to be made about policy outcomes, rather than building a tight case about success or failure.

From his Australian experience in federal policy evaluation, Mackay (2004) observed that greater independence and objectivity of evaluation often reduced the buy-in by the 'line' department that was being evaluated. It may be that self-evaluations have a better access to what happened, but typically the central agencies see these as being less independent and objective. The use of evaluations by the Department of Finance peaked in the 1990s, and they now receive less attention. 'Line' departments have tended to use evaluations to argue for ongoing funds, rather than applying the evaluation lessons to the next policy iteration, as the classical policy cycle would hope.

Then Auditor-General Ian McPhee (McPhee, 2006) spoke to the different roles of evaluation and audit. Unlike a performance audit, an evaluation can look at policy merit, but it may be perceived as less independent.

A 'performance audit' is an independent review of the efficiency or administrative effectiveness of a program or agency under the *Auditor-General Act 1997*. Performance audits of environment programs have frowned over the meaningfulness of the stated program outcomes. For example, auditors recognised that a Natural Heritage Trust output indicator such as 'kilometres of fence constructed per annum' doesn't really say much one way or the other about 'enhanced biodiversity protection'. Indirectly, however, audits of federal environment programs do provide clues about drivers of success. They laud clear and measurable objectives, consultation with stakeholders; and central agency scrutiny for policy proposals.

While program evaluations and audits have their limitations, they are useful tools to establish or confirm with some degree of objectivity what did or not what work in policy. They are often consulted in this book and they inform its case studies.

Beyond the strictures of evaluations, what does the research say about measuring policy 'success'? Does it offer any tools that can be used to assess the veracity of policy 'successes' or 'failures' that might be nominated by practising officials at interviews?

There is an established literature on policy success/failure and policy learning, in developing and transitional economies, an early example being the work on anticipating failure by Grindle (1981). However, until recently, the concept of success in policymaking in advanced economies with stable Westminster governments has received surprisingly little attention.

Among this recent work, the chosen guide here was Marsh and McConnell (2010) with McConnell (2010a, 2010b). They confronted the underlying issues of meaning and intention in policy success, asserting that, "policy success is nothing more than a social construct that reflects power relations". They tried to rise above the protracted debates in the literature on positivism versus interpretivism, and whether or not the policy cycle is a useful heuristic.

Table 2.3: Dimensions of policy success as identified by Marsh and McConnell

Dimensions	Indicators
Process	Legitimacy in the formation of choices: that is, produced through due processes of constitutional and quasi-constitutional procedures and values of democracy, deliberation and accountability
	Passage of legislation: was the legislation passed with no, or few, amendments?
	Political sustainability: did the policy have the support of a sufficient coalition?
	Innovation and influence: was the policy based on new ideas or policy instruments, or did it involve the adoption of policy from elsewhere (policy transfer/diffusion)?
Programmatic	Operational: was it implemented as per objectives?
	Outcome: did it achieve the intended outcomes?
	Resource: was it an efficient use of resources?
	Actor/interest: did the policy/implementation benefit a particular class, interest group, alliance, political party, gender, race, religion, territorial community, institution, ideology, etc.?
Political	Government popularity: is the policy politically popular?
	Did it help government's re-election/election chances?
	Did it help secure or boost its credibility?

McConnell argued for 'success' as a fresh construct to understand policy. This allows theorists to incorporate the chaotic, irrational and fast-paced world of politics, a key to understanding policy, but rarely addressed in policy theory (McConnell, 2010b, 220). With Marsh, McConnell has explored the conditions necessary to foster and sustain policy success, and the negotiation and engagement strategies adopted by policy officials. Both thought it important to judge in practical terms the success or failure of policies, and they proposed criteria for so doing. Their 'Marsh and McConnell Framework' (Marsh and McConnell, 2010, 570-571) in Table 2.3 proposes three dimensions of policy success – process, programmatic and political – with several indicators for each.

Other scholars have readily taken up Marsh and McConnell's invitation for researchers to refine their framework. Van Assche et al. (2011) analysed unjustified Netherlands Government claims of 'policy success' in land use planning. The UK Institute of Government (Rutter et al., 2012) applied the Framework in a major program of research into six successful UK policies. Crowley and Walker (2012, 8) saw merit in applying a modified version of the Framework to case studies of Australian environment policy failure. This early adoption suggests the framework is resonating with theorists attempting to understand different aspects of policy success.

The Framework guided this book at several points. To begin with, it focused the interviews on reflections about environment policy success, rather than recollections of environment policy failure. Secondly, the indicators in the Framework offered a rubric that could be used to check externally the validity of interviewee assessments of program success or failure, particularly in the case of the 12 policies or programs given particular attention (Table 1.5). These external checks are illustrated in Chapter 3 and again in Chapter 5, which case studies selected policies and programs that the interviewees judged to be successes or failures. Then Chapter 6 discusses possible refinements of the Framework.

Chapter 3
Success and Failure in Australian Environment Policies

In order to explore environment policy success and failure, this chapter explains the choice of the research design, semi-structured interviews with senior policy officials.

It lays out the process for selecting the interviewees, the nature and adequacy of the sample, and the ground covered by the interview questions.

The insiders' assessments of policy success and failure are tabulated and analysed, especially for the 12 target programs and policies. For these 12, the insider assessments are validated against external assessments derived by applying the Marsh and McConnell Framework. A particular interest is why the opinions diverge on some programs but converge (either on program success or program failure) for others.

3.1 The research paradigm

The research question prompting this book was whether or not policy success was a useful construct to understand policymaking. Two sub questions sprang from this. Do policy officials have a prior sense of whether or not a policy is likely to succeed? What are the key factors likely to drive policy success?

Public policy theorists debate the best paradigm for theorising about what works in public policy. Lindblom (1959, 1979) wrote of policy in terms of "muddling through", after discussions with practitioners. Schön (1995, 18) recognised that part of the role of the policy analyst is to reduce "messes" to manageable plans and, indeed, to "find the right problem" in the first place. Wildavsky (1979, 15) and Goodin (1982, 248) saw policy as an art and craft as much as a science. Yanow (1996, 6) argued that too many descriptions of the policy process are shaped by the assumption that all human action is rational. In her view, every step is imbued with meaning arising from the experiences, beliefs and values of the policy researcher and the policymaker. Stewart and Jones (2003) and Stewart (2009) argued that policy is best recognised as a political act that always involves an expression of values.

Yanow is the touchstone here, as she sought to bridge the positivist and interpretivist worlds of policy analysis. Three points she made guide this study. First, she argued that the diversity of views and values doesn't mean that you don't try to understand or undertake policy. Rather, the task of analysis is to uncover and understand the reality of these multiple interpretations (Yanow, 1996, 234). Second, she was nervous about universal theories, and argued that the diversity of views and values calls for context-specific knowledge and situation-specific research. Finally, she argued that implementation cannot be viewed in simple success or failure terms, as these need to be understood in terms of what they mean to the actors involved.

Before this project finally settled on a research plan and method, it considered earlier studies that had approached similar research questions. Would this project be a broad-brush quantitative study or a qualitative in-depth study, would it focus on policy officials only or a broader set of policy agents, and which data-gathering tools would be used?

Large-scale, high-level studies of differing aspects of policy success reinforced the author's judgment to access the *insider* perspective in *specific* cases. Baumgartner and Jones (2009) spent many years tracing the trajectories of seven large policies (such as nuclear power, urban planning, smoking, auto safety and child abuse) on the American political radar. At this grand scale, they were reliant on data from external sources, mainly changes in budget allocations, but also analyses of interest groups, media reports, published studies and congressional committee activity. This 'outsider' perspective limited the insights they could generate on how policy agendas are set.

Harmelink et al. (2008) sought to identify predictors of success for 20 energy efficiency policies in Europe, relying on published monitoring. Although they sought to verify their theory through interviews with policymakers, their study highlighted the limitations of large-scale studies across differing policy domains and jurisdictions.

The sheer breadth of these studies, and their lack of access to officials, makes it difficult to unpack the links between policy intents and outcomes.

The qualitative approaches adopted by Kingdon (2003), Althaus (2004), Middle (2010) and others are preferred here. Kingdon (2003, 231-232) generated ground-breaking theory on agenda setting. He did detailed in-depth interviews with US government officials, supported by analysis of public records. He compared two policy areas, to limit the risk that his generalisations about policy agenda setting might be due to idiosyncrasies of one policy area. Through his interview techniques, he was able to uncover much about the intent, motivations and strategies of the government officials.

Althaus (2008) researched political risk calculations, and the implications of political risk assessments for policy design. To examine how politicians, the media and policy officials determine whether a policy is politically risky, she looked at a mix of domestic and international policy crises, supported by in-depth interviews.

Similarly, in WA Government environment policymaking, Middle (2010, iii) employed qualitative case studies and interviews to investigate which policymaking approach (expert-driven regulatory, participatory or collaborative) was most likely to deliver success. He concluded that an "adaptive-collaborative" approach was the most likely to succeed, when stakeholder conflict is high (Middle, 2010, 183-184).

Page and Jenkins (2005) is a rare empirical study that looks to the policy official. This duo argued that accessing the work of policy necessitated delving deeper, to talk to the mid-ranking officials seen to do the 'heavy lifting'. They conducted 20-minute interviews with a tiny (128) sample out of more than 100,000 mid-ranking officials spread across 13 UK government agencies. Their interview questions were simply "What do you do?" and "How did you come to be in this job?"

Page and Jenkins is one model for this study, despite their small sample and methodological limitations. They acknowledged they were missing the insights of higher-level officials or politicians. As 't Hart (2007) put it, Page and Jenkins couldn't build up a granular understanding of any one policy episode or how it evolved. But they offered, he conceded, a rare insight into the largely unstudied world of policy officials.

The very breadth of the broad-brush comparative policy studies dilutes their scope to understand the policy process. Conversely, the narrower scope of Kingdon, Althaus, or Middle plays up how the policy arises, the policy design, and the policy outcomes. The preference here to go in-depth into one policy agency (and one policy field, environment) might mean a loss of comparative analysis, but it might provide a deeper analysis of the drivers of success in Australian federal environment policy.

The assumption here is that 'policy' is much more than the official record of government decisions. The decision itself is not the key. It is how that decision came to be taken and how it was given effect, matters that are opaque to the external observer. This study didn't want to be one of "academics on the outside

47

looking in" as it was put by the Canadian, Williams (2010, 200). "Academics are acutely aware that they have limited access to government documents, people and processes," he remarked, "particularly the core artefacts that help move policy forward; that is to government documents, people and processes."

3.2 The research design

The interplay between endogenous and exogenous factors in policymaking makes it hard to prove that policy variables 'cause' policy outcomes. This study was meant to explore the probabilities of differing policy outcomes. That called for a design that could accommodate ambiguities and contradictions in the evidence (Denzin and Lincoln, 2003, x, New York University, 2011, 11).

The review of the theoretical literature in the previous chapter confirmed that no single theoretical framework was fully suited to frame the study. Tellingly, neither Kingdon nor Page and Jenkins began their studies with a fixed set of hypotheses derived from a theoretical framework. Similarly, this study did not begin with a set analytical framework. Rather, it was to rely mainly on the interviews, to extract the officials' experience of what works or fails in environment policymaking.

The literature recognises the value in accessing 'insider perspectives' (Althaus, 2004, Barrett, 2004, Castles, 2004, Colebatch, 2007, Feldman, 1989, Nevill, 2007). In this study, in-depth semi-structured interviews with key environment policymakers were selected as the primary data collection, supported by reference to publicly available information (budget documents, evaluations, audits, research), and also a detailed consideration of 12 targeted programs and policies (Table 1.5). The active ingredients underlying the research questions are the observations and actions of the policy officials – are they able to identify indicators of likely success or failure?

As an alternative to the interviews, questionnaire or survey approaches were considered. These failed the test of alignment with the subjective nature of policymaking, and they would not have enabled follow up questions or 'prompt' questions. Moreover, neither would enable an easy tailoring of the process to the seniority of each interviewee.

The five-step research design adopted for this study is outlined below.

Figure 3.1: The five-step research pathway

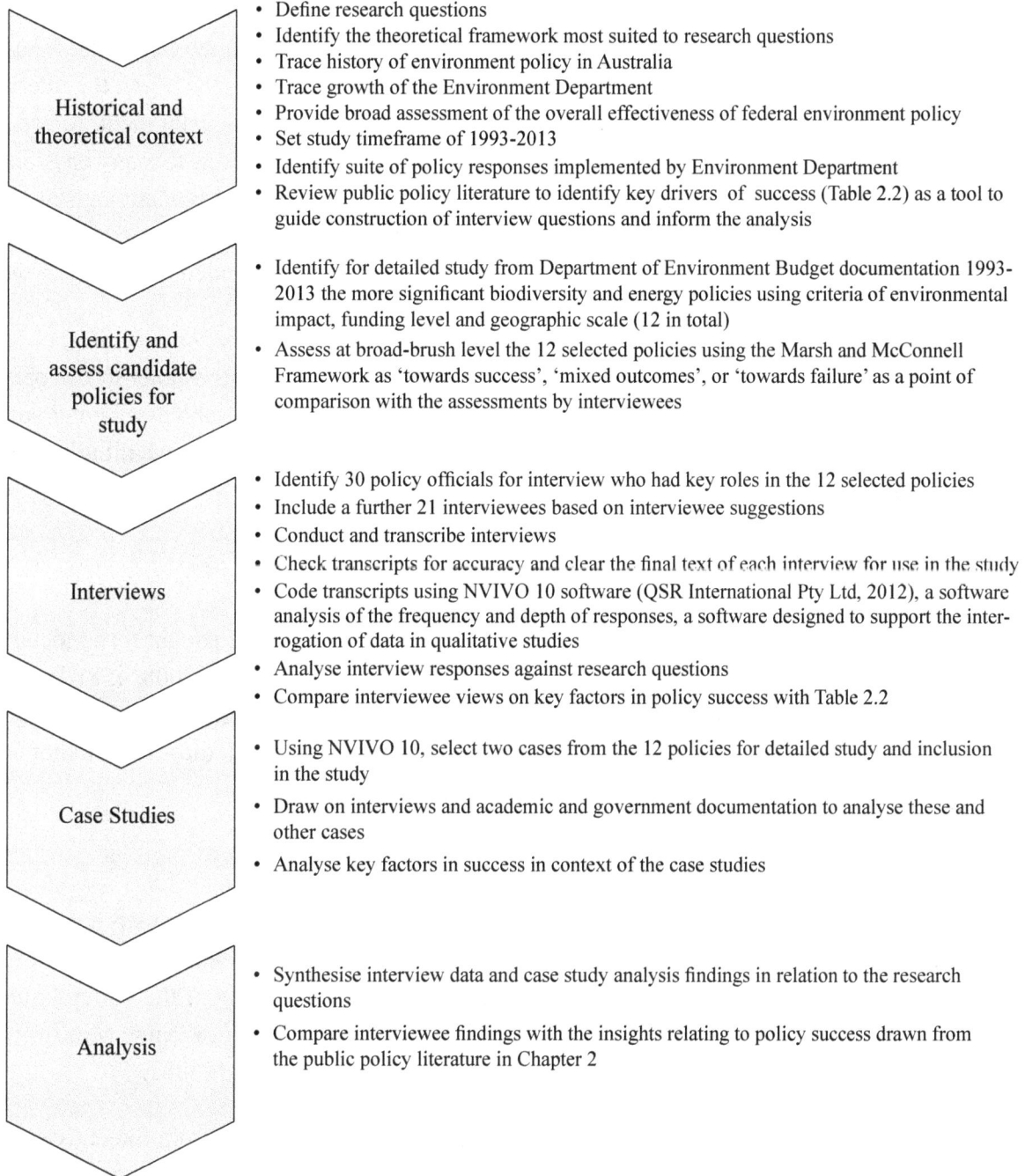

Historical and theoretical context

- Define research questions
- Identify the theoretical framework most suited to research questions
- Trace history of environment policy in Australia
- Trace growth of the Environment Department
- Provide broad assessment of the overall effectiveness of federal environment policy
- Set study timeframe of 1993-2013
- Identify suite of policy responses implemented by Environment Department
- Review public policy literature to identify key drivers of success (Table 2.2) as a tool to guide construction of interview questions and inform the analysis

Identify and assess candidate policies for study

- Identify for detailed study from Department of Environment Budget documentation 1993-2013 the more significant biodiversity and energy policies using criteria of environmental impact, funding level and geographic scale (12 in total)
- Assess at broad-brush level the 12 selected policies using the Marsh and McConnell Framework as 'towards success', 'mixed outcomes', or 'towards failure' as a point of comparison with the assessments by interviewees

Interviews

- Identify 30 policy officials for interview who had key roles in the 12 selected policies
- Include a further 21 interviewees based on interviewee suggestions
- Conduct and transcribe interviews
- Check transcripts for accuracy and clear the final text of each interview for use in the study
- Code transcripts using NVIVO 10 software (QSR International Pty Ltd, 2012), a software analysis of the frequency and depth of responses, a software designed to support the interrogation of data in qualitative studies
- Analyse interview responses against research questions
- Compare interviewee views on key factors in policy success with Table 2.2

Case Studies

- Using NVIVO 10, select two cases from the 12 policies for detailed study and inclusion in the study
- Draw on interviews and academic and government documentation to analyse these and other cases
- Analyse key factors in success in context of the case studies

Analysis

- Synthesise interview data and case study analysis findings in relation to the research questions
- Compare interviewee findings with the insights relating to policy success drawn from the public policy literature in Chapter 2

As Figure 3.1 indicates, the research process was iterative.

'Programs', not 'policies', were the initial focus, because funded programs are a common way of looking at chunks of policy (McConnell, 2010a, 347). On completion of the interviews, the focus was broadened to include national strategies and legislation. This was for two reasons. First, the interviews confirmed that the national environment strategies (ecologically sustainable development, forests, bio-diversity, marine and population) as listed at Table 1.4 were critical underpinnings to many environment programs. Also, many interviewees drew good examples from the primary environment legislation (the *EPBC Act 1999*) or from the *Fuel Quality Standards Act 2000*, in their discussions of policy success and failure. Hence, the final list targeted for closer attention (Table 1.5) included 'policies' as well as 'programs'.

Also, in view of the depth of the interview responses, the initial research questions in the previous section were broadened to include a consideration of how the officials went about pursuing success. Similarly, the number of interviews grew from a planned 30 to 51, due to the 'snowballing' effect that is discussed below.

3.3 Interviewing the policy officials

As the research was looking at policymaking from the insider perspective, it sought respondents who could speak with genuine authority about the policymaking experience (Bryman, 2008, 458). Interviewees also had to have had a primary role in one or more of the 12 selected programs or policies. The interviews were to include a mix of experiences in programs or policies that both did – and did not – meet their stated objectives.

Selecting the officials for interview

In the Australian Public Service (APS), experienced Executive Level 1 and 2 officers typically undertake the policy development, also Band 1 (Branch Head) officers, with occasional guidance from Band 2 officers. The Secretary and the Deputy Secretaries can get involved directly, if the policy issues are highly political, complex, and problematic, or of acute interest to the Minister or Prime Minister. Band 1 officers right through to Secretaries, all of these may draft policy from time to time.

Therefore, the officers initially identified for interview ranged across all levels from Executive Level 1 up to Secretary. This served to counter the Page and Jenkins (2005, 180) criticism of an undue focus on policy 'elites'.

50

The interviews included *all five* of the Secretaries who ran the Department from 1993 through to September 2013, and the majority (nine) of the Deputy Secretaries. This ensured the inclusion of officials who had access to Ministers and their offices, and were accountable for the implementation of Cabinet policy decisions through Senate Estimates, and indeed through their own performance agreements. It addressed the concerns expressed by 't Hart (2007) that insider research which excluded high level officials would miss out on subtler issues of power, exchange and conflict.

Table 3.1: Department of Environment, job levels, number interviewed, and pay rates, July 2012

Term used in this study	Job level and terms used	Number interviewed	Pay rate at 1/7/2012
Tier 1	Secretary Department Head	5	Over $500,000
	Band 3 Deputy Secretary	9	Over $350,000
Tier 2	Band 2 First Assistant Secretary Division Head	7	Over $275,000
	Band 1 (1) Assistant Secretary Branch Head Group Manager	10	Over $220,000
Tier 3	Executive Level 2 Director Section Head	12	$115,000 to $134,000
	Executive Level 1 Assistant Director Senior Policy Officer	8	$98,000 to $105,000
Total		51	

(1) All positions at Band 1 and above belong to the APS 'Senior Executive Service' (SES).

In this study, the APS terms themselves are largely avoided. They are confusing and several terms may apply to a single level. For example, the APS 'Executive' Levels 1 and 2 are low in the hierarchy compared with a business executive. An SES 'Band 2' may also be known as a First Assistant Secretary or Division Head. To circumvent this confusion, but acknowledge the relevance of an interviewee's place in the APS hierarchy, interviewees are referred to from here on as 'Tier 1' down to 'Tier 2' and 'Tier 3'. Table 3.1 explains these tiers and their (then) pay rates.

Thirty potential interviewees were initially identified as meeting the criterion of extensive experience in the 12 programs and policies selected for attention. Knowing the principal author, and assured of anonymity, all agreed to be interviewed. After the 30th interview, answers to the research questions began to emerge with a sense of convergence in the findings. Each interviewee had added at least one unique insight. They also suggested an additional 21 interviewees, who would in their view contribute to the study. All were duly added, and again all agreed to be interviewed. The interview process thus had an unanticipated 'snowballing' effect. After the 51st interview, there seemed to be diminishing value in further interviews.

Participants were selected to ensure a balanced sample by level and by sex. Importantly, they also represented a range of experiences in success and failure across significant environment programs and policies delivered by the Department over the study period. The final sample of 51 officials included 26 males and 25 females, spread across all three tiers. Thirty-one officers were at Tiers 1-2, an estimated 40 per cent of all the Tiers 1-2 who were involved in the targeted programs and policies over 1993-2013.

Taken together, the sample of interviewees comprises a breadth and depth of experience in federal policymaking that is rarely captured in academic studies. Fifty-one is greater than the number of officials interviewed either by Althaus (2004) or Middle (2010). Palmer (2007) based his study of immigration policy on just eight interviews, one Prime Minister, four Ministers, and three public servants.

Given the study's prerequisite of significant policy experience, over 30 interviewees had more than 15 years' experience in environment policy, in the Environment Department or elsewhere. Six held over 30 years' experience. Only seven had less than five years in environment policy. Five of these had specialist skills. Two had joined the Department at a high level after lengthy experience in other agencies. Sixty-five per cent of interviewees were still with the Department. Another 14 per cent were elsewhere inside the APS and 22 per cent were outside or retired.

Nearly 75 per cent of interviewees had been involved in Cabinet, budget or ministerial processes. They had diverse experience across many policy areas of the Environment Department. At least ten interviewees had had exposure to one or the other of Greens Loans, Home Insulation, Fuel Quality, solar programs, park management, Caring for Our Country, marine policies, Natural Heritage Trust, Regional Forest Agreements, water policies, pollution control, and the *EPBC Act*.

Compiling and analysing the interviews

The interviews canvassed the following questions. Which policies were considered to have been particularly successful? Is it possible to predict success? What are key factors driving policy success and failure? Where do policy proposals come from? What influences policy design? Interviewees were asked to describe at least one policy experience in which they had a key role, but they could also refer to others. Again, the full set of interview questions is at the Appendix.

Interviews were face-to-face and flexible. Not all questions were asked of each interviewee. Questions were tailored to experience and seniority, especially where the officer had specialised experience or was very high-level. Some interviewees spoke at length without questions, in which case the question list was used to check that all topics had been covered. Interviewees were prompted for information or clarification when necessary, with impromptu questions to follow up new issues that might emerge.

The principal author was the interviewer. She transcribed all interviews, which were offered to interviewees for checking. Forty made no changes. Others made minor changes.

The principal author worked in the Environment Department from 1995 to 2009, at SES level from 1997 onwards. She had direct working experience of many of the programs and policies under discussion. This background gave her access and trust with interviewees, and a ready understanding of the technicalities and the jargon.

Such a researcher may tend to be protective of her former organisation and colleagues, or overplay the importance of their role. The risk of 'capture' was lessened by the interviews being conducted three years after her departure from the Department. More importantly, the analysis and findings were subject to numerous checks and balances.

The analysis of the interviews kept in mind Schwartz-Shea and Yanow's (2012, 33) injunction for interpretive researchers "to retain an openness to the possibility of surprises as well as to resist the 'rush to diagnosis' that prematurely closes down analytical possibilities". The analysis often employs direct quotes, mainly to highlight views that were frequently expressed or particularly insightful, and occasionally to capture interesting outliers or contrarian opinions.

To lend numerical rigour to the interpretive and qualitative analysis, the 'Numbers' software was used to test for relationships between interviewee profiles and interviewee responses, while the 'NVIVO 10' software was used to group and analyse the data, to ensure a systematic consideration of all interview responses, and to control for interview bias. This extra work confirmed that variations of opinion correlated rather more with the interviewees' tier and breadth of policy experience, rather less with everyday factors such as their sex or their numerical years of experience.

To balance the focus on policy officials, the analysis drew on public assessments of policy and program outcomes gleaned from the wider literature (reviews, evaluations, inquiries, and other published research findings). These were particularly valuable for Working on Country and the Home Insulation Program.

Six other senior policy officials, who were not involved in the interviews, checked the draft findings for plausibility and consistency.

Findings related to success, or failure, of the 12 target policies and programs were also corroborated by comparing to findings for the same programs derived externally by applying the Marsh and McConnell Framework (Table 2.3). Among other things, this helped to control for any 'participation bias' that might incline interviewees to up-rate policies that they themselves had worked on.

3.4 Insider assessments of policy success

As a lead-in to more complex interview questions on what drives policy success, all interviewees were asked simply: Which federal environment policies or programs do you think have been particularly successful? The answers to this open-ended question referred to a wide range of programs and policies implemented by the Department over the study period.

The 51 interviewees rated a total of 38 programs and policies for success or failure. This full suite of programs and policies referred to by interviewees as succeeding (or failing) is set out in Figure 3.2 (and Figure 3.3 below). For comparative purposes, this includes programs and policies not in the target 12, including a few that began before the study timeframe of 1993-2013, also a few that only received one nomination.

By inspection, 22 of these initiatives were always rated successful, with no negative nominations. These only appear in Figure 3.2. Six were 'mixed', or successful for some interviewees but not others. These appear in both Figure 3.2 and 3.3. Ten were always rated failed, and only appear in Figure 3.3.

Figure 3.2: All policies nominated as *successful* by interviewees

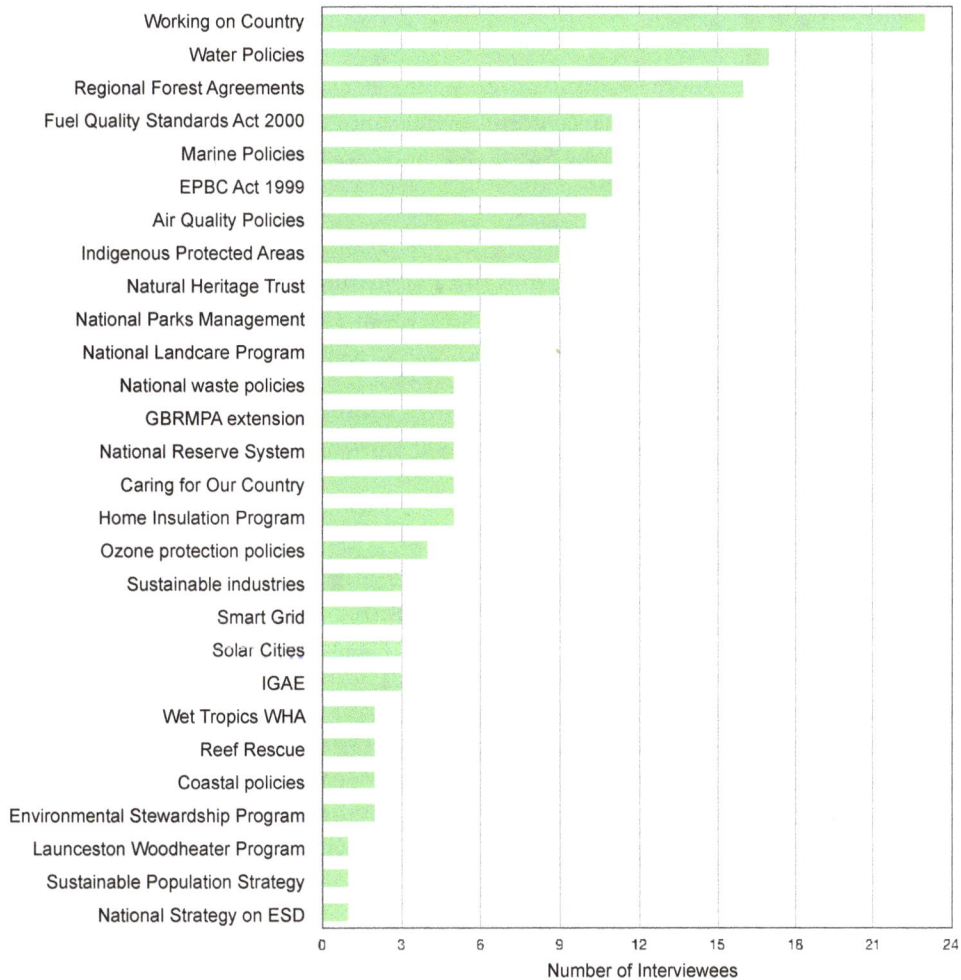

In the first or always-successful category, Working on Country was nominated as successful 23 times with no failure nominations. Its forerunner program, Indigenous Protected Areas, received nine success nominations and no fails. In between sat Fuel Quality Standards, with 11 successes and no fails.

The case study of Working on Country boils its success down to proper resources for wages and on-costs, engaged stakeholders, a clear biodiversity rationale plus political appeal, and crafty design. Chapter 5 has more details.

All six policies in the 'mixed' category were large and complex initiatives. Regional Forest Agreements and Marine Protected Areas were mostly rated successful with a few negatives. Opinions were more evenly divided on the *EPBC Act*, Natural Heritage Trust and Caring for Our Country.

The Home Insulation Program attracted by far the highest number of failure nominations, 18. Interviewees pointed to unrealistic timeframes, weak oversight, mismatch between staff recruitment decisions and required skills for several critical positions, poor risk management, confusing economic and 'green' objectives, and poor handling of ministers and stakeholders.

The program severely damaged Federal Labor, and the Department's reputation, prompting numerous inquiries plus a Royal Commission. As late as 2015, the Abbott Government was still advertising compensation for insulation firms adversely affected in 2009-10. Nevertheless, Table 3.3 shows that five interviewees rated the program successful, insisting that it stimulated the economy and insulated 1.1 million homes, with the attendant energy efficiency gains. More details on Home Insulation are in the Chapter 5 case study.

The *EPBC Act 1999* received the second highest number of failure nominations, nine out of 20 ratings. Most Tier 1-2s thought the Act successful, to the extent that, for the first time ever, it gave the federal Environment Minister decision-making powers on matters of national significance.

Lower-tier interviewees were more inclined to be sceptical about the effectiveness of the Act on the ground. Their jaundiced view is lent credence by the recent compilation (Milman and Evershed, 2015) that over 97 per cent of all mining or resource projects ever reviewed under EPBC have reverted to the default setting, in other words, "approval with conditions". Very few assessable projects have ever been knocked back.

All three tiers saw the Act as comprehensively failing to protect endangered species. A Tier 1 interviewee severely regretted the unbalanced focus on "charismatic species":

> 'The focus on individual species recovery plans was, I thought, conceptually wrong. As an economist I would rather have a triage system, where you acknowledge that some species are in god's waiting room. Much to my irritation, [recovery plans for individual species] was a big focus under the Act.'

Regional Forest Agreements split opinion, if less so than *EPBC*. One the one hand, the 16 interviewees who rated it successful were referring very much to its damping of the political tension between the conservationists and the logging industry. As one put it:

Figure 3.3: All policies nominated as *failing* by interviewees

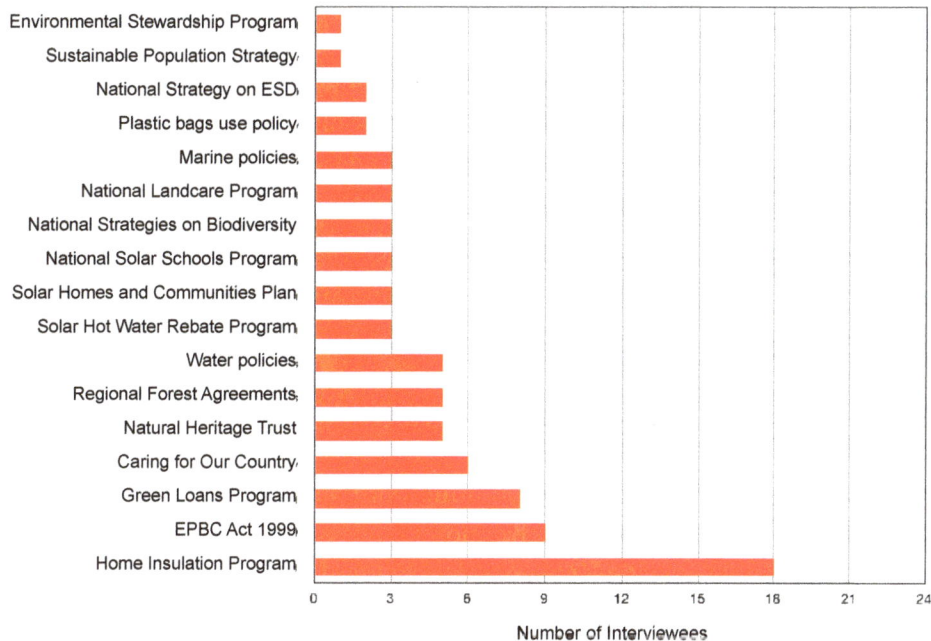

'The overall objective of the RFA process, unstated by the Federal Government, I always thought was to get the issue off the front pages and get the Commonwealth Government out of day-to-day management and so in that sense it was spectacularly successful. But that is not necessarily an outcome for an environmental purpose.'

On the other hand, the five who assessed RFAs as failed thought the process had delivered a political outcome at the cost of sound environmental outcomes. Essentially, they perceived the same picture as the 16 optimistic assessments, but they put less weight on the political 'success' and more on the environmental failure.

With eight nominations for failure and none for success, a standout program in the third or always-failed category was the Green Loans program, a Rudd Government initiative to subsidise home sustainability assessments and the interest payments on loans for 'green' home renovations. Interviewees described a low quality product, an over-engineered program design but with very poor management of demand, plus a serious case of financial mismanagement.

The Solar Hot Water Rebate Scheme, National Solar Schools Program, and Solar Homes and Communities Plan, each received three failure nominations and no successes. Their popular appeal was overshadowed by inequity, high unit costs of emissions reduction, uncontrolled demand, and safety issues.

The interviews show the officials as capable of making reasonable, and reasonably objective, distinctions between program successes and program failures, assessments that are not merely reflections of their degree of association with the program. Where the officials are 'mixed' in their views, this is partly a reflection of mixed outcomes in the programs themselves. But it is also a reflection of their differing experience and outlooks. This is notable with the *EPBC Act* and Regional Forest Agreements. While higher-level officials are inclined to approve these programs for their Canberra political 'success', lower officials look more to their lack of success in the field.

Successful 'brown' programs versus failing 'green' programs

Nine interviewees put another slant on success, pointing out that 'brown' or pollution control policies (ozone, air, water, and fuel quality) tended to be more successful than 'green' or biodiversity policies such as the *EPBC Act,* Caring for Our Country, the Natural Heritage Trust, and Regional Marine Planning.

National Fuel Quality Standards, though low in profile, appeared to be a 'win-win', delivering major economic and health benefits, as well as environment benefits, through reduced vehicle emissions. Interviewees referred to it as 'the greatest impact of all environment programs' and 'the biggest [environment] policy success in terms of objective outcomes'. See Chapter 5 for more details on this initiative.

Conversely, interviewees commonly said that biodiversity policies were overrated, as they didn't make a tangible or lasting difference to overall biodiversity protection, as distinct from simply meeting 'random' or scientifically arbitrary targets for species representation in isolated 'patches' of protected areas.

3.5 Reality-checking the insider assessments

Table 3.2: Targeted environment programs and policies 1993-2013: success-failure per Marsh and McConnell Framework versus success-failure per interviewees

Program or policy	Interviewees' success/ failure nominations	
	Success	Failure
Rated towards success under M & McC (1)		
Working on Country (2)	23	0
Fuel Quality Standards Act 2000	9	0
Rated mixed outcomes under M & McC (1)		
Natural Heritage Trust	9	5
Regional Forest Agreements	16	5
EPBC Act 1999	11	9
Marine Protected Areas	11	3
Caring for Our Country	5	6
Rated towards failure under M & McC (1)		
Home Insulation Program	5	18
Green Loans Program	0	8
Solar Homes & Communities Plan	0	3
Solar Hot Water Rebate Program	0	3
National Solar Schools Program	0	3

(1) Towards success means broadly successful on all three Marsh & McConnell (M & McC) dimensions of process, programmatic and political; mixed outcomes means neither outstandingly successful nor unsuccessful on any one dimension but no major failings; towards failure means broadly failed across all three dimensions.

(2) Rows add to < 51, as interviewees generally stuck to programs they had direct knowledge of.

Table 3.2 compares interviewee success-failure ratings, for the targeted 12 programs and policies, with the corresponding ratings derived by applying the three dimensions of the Marsh and McConnell Framework. Examples of how the ratings were derived appear in Chapter 5. The case studies in that chapter consider the process, program and political dimensions for Fuel Standards and Working on Country (successful) and Home Insulation and Sustainable Population Strategy (failure).

In Table 3.2, the Framework ratings readily align with the interviewee ratings, with the partial exception of Home Insulation. This slid towards failure on all three dimensions of the Framework, given its dire execution, failure to measure outcomes against the stated environmental objectives, four installer deaths, and long-lasting political fallout.

Eighteen interviewees concurred but, as noted above, five interviewees disagreed with the majority, discounting the political fallout in favour of the stimulus effect.

Although not included in Table 3.2, and rarely mentioned by interviewees, the Sustainable Population Strategy (Commonwealth of Australia, 2011) was a significant failure, and is treated in more detail in Chapter 5. It is analogous to the Home Insulation Program. That is, senior officers disagreed on its success or failure, but the Framework points to failure.

One SES officer strongly repudiated the Population Strategy, as do-nothing policy "getting the issue off the political agenda" for the minister. For very much the same reasons, another perceived it as a success. It is a stretch to reach the latter conclusion, by any reasonable application of the dimensions in the Framework, as Chapter 5 will show.

While the sample of 12 programs and policies is not large, it nevertheless represents a significant slice of the Environment Department's initiatives over 1993-2013, and (Table 1.5) a total all-years investment of around $10 billion. While the sample of 'insider' officials is not large, it is unusually comprehensive for a research study, and it represents a significant slice of all the senior officials who were ever involved in Environment Department policy over 1993-2013.

Within the merits of this particular sample of programs and officials, it seems that what the Framework tends to correct for is narrow assessments of success or failure that place undue weight on any one of the process, programmatic or political dimensions.

For example, where quite a number of officials are inclined to approve of RFAs or the *EPBC Act* for their 'political' success, the Framework turns the attention back to their 'programmatic' or environmental failures. Conversely, where some senior officials tend to endorse the 'programmatic' or economic outcomes of Home Insulation, the Framework has little choice but to wrap in its glaring political and process failures.

In summary, Table 3.2 confirms the merit of 'externally' assessing programs for success or failure by application of the Marsh and McConnell Framework. This adds weight to other applications of the Framework since 2010, and suggests that it is worth further investigation. Both inside and outside academe, there is relatively little work on the important social policy question of what constitutes program success or failure, and it is too easy to make claims either way on a narrow or partisan basis.

Chapter 4

Predictors of Success or Failure for Environment Policy

This chapter reviews what the interviewees said about the predictive factors for successful policy outcomes, in comparison with what the policy literature says.

The interviewees prioritised three critical factors for policy success also highlighted in the literature – consulting stakeholders, clear objectives, and clear evidence. In their work, they approached these factors differently to the normative literature. Mindful of the dominance of economics, officials were wont to package the objectives and evidence so as to maximise their transient environment policy opportunities.

The interviewees played down other key success factors – adequacy of resources, policy origins, and policy design – emphasised in the policy literature. They rather favoured two other factors that are less well studied. These were the extent (or otherwise) of the policy mandate and, most important of all, the degree of policy agency exercised (or not) by officials.

4.1 Predictors of policy success: practitioners versus the theory

The first research question in this study was about whether or not policy officials have a prior sense of whether a policy is likely to succeed, and if so on what basis.

The interview results showed that the officials did not explicitly think about success, but primarily sought to avoid failure. Their predictions of success or failure were intuitive and instinctual, rather than derived from an orderly, systematic framework.

Nevertheless, the literature quite reasonably calls for a more systematic approach to understanding what does or does not work in policymaking. The same question was at the forefront of this research.

Therefore, interviewees were also asked the direct question: *What are the key factors that need to be in place to achieve a successful environment policy?*

Leaving aside exogenous factors, and the critical role that the Environment Minister can play, the interview responses generated a consistent set of key factors thought necessary to achieve policy success.

Only one of the 51 interviewees gave an almost textbook response to the question of what drives policy success: the problem to be solved is defined and understood and supported by solid information; the policy response is carefully designed to address the problem; and the policy response can be adaptively adjusted in implementation.

Table 4.1: Factors predictive of policy success, as nominated by the interviewees

Success factors	Citations
Securing stakeholder buy-in and support	30
Ensuring clarity of rationale and objectives	29
Having sufficient time to create policy opportunities and for implementation	20
Securing the evidence to support and defend the policy	16
Understanding the level of political and departmental Executive commitment	14
Securing support from the other agencies, including central agencies	13
Carving out a clear role for the Commonwealth and with the States onside	12
Securing the right personnel to develop and administer	12
Link the environment policy to economic benefits	11
Developing a clear, simple, compelling narrative for Ministers and the public	10
Engage in policy design as early as possible	9
Securing sufficient resources including for structural adjustment and for staff	9

Table 4.1: Factors predictive of policy success, as nominated by the interviewees (cont.)

Success factors	Citations
A robust process to identify all dimensions of the issue and options	8
Developing a sound policy or legislative framework with consistent principles	6
Measuring visible outcomes to demonstrate a difference has been made	4
Identifying any unintended consequences	4
Trialing at smaller scale first to test and tailor policy settings	4
Understanding of the political motivations and constraints in the context of the electoral cycle	3
Understand what policy levers you have at your disposal	3
Developing robust processes for planning, data and project management	3
Securing strong Executive leadership in the Department	3
Securing funds for structural adjustment if needed	2
Ensuring clarity over winners and losers	2
Building in the potential for adaptive management in implementation	2

Ranking the success factors according to the number of citations, Table 4.1 captures the breadth of interviewee responses. Of all the success factors, the most commonly cited (30 times) was the need to build a coalition of support for the policy among stakeholder interests. Such interests went beyond those directly impacted by the policy, including also the degree of support from politicians, the departmental Executive, other Commonwealth agencies and especially the central agencies, and State Government agencies.

The next most common set of factors (29 citations) was the need for a clear understanding of the issue with clear objectives supported by evidence, followed by sufficient time for implementation (20), evidence that supported the policy (16), and the level of commitment in the Government and in the Department (14).

Stakeholder support, clarity of objectives, and use of evidence, are prominent here, as they also are in the policy literature, as summarised at Table 2.2. On closer study, the interviewees interpret these three factors differently to the way they are presented in the literature.

For example, interviewees cited Australia's strong consultation processes within government, as compared with how such processes work in other countries. They thought it was essential for environmental policies to have support from the internal stakeholders, meaning their Departmental Executive, the central agencies of Australian Government, and other federal agencies.

For them, however, consulting with external stakeholders was not just about the conventional discussion and negotiation of priorities.

Often it involved, as one put it, "sharply divided and competing sets of interests". To span these divisions, interviewees sought to understand extreme views, by bringing "the enemy into the camp" and "covering off the losers". That commonly meant financial compensation to those negatively affected. Of course, this ploy also has recent parallels in Australian climate change policy.

Consultation could at times be studied or disingenuous, as was implied in more than half of the interviewee responses. At such times, it could be undertaken at a distance, or with those not directly affected by the policy, or (as in Caring for our Country) after the key decisions were already set. In practice then, 'stakeholder consultation' assumed subtle colorations that are not well represented in the literature.

Similarly, the interview transcripts put a different construction on the use of clear evidence as the logical link between issue and solution. This proposition is almost axiomatic in the literature.

In the case of Fuel Quality Standards, there was a rare alignment between the economic and environmental cases for the new policy. New vehicle technologies, hitherto ruled out by the lack of national fuel standards, could also lower emissions and reduce pollution.

A more common pattern in the interviews was a deliberate blurring of the environmental objectives, which were not seen to have immediate appeal, so as to prioritise the economic or social aims, which were. A positive example of this pattern was the Working on Country program. Its policy architects wanted to secure funding for activities that might better protect biodiversity in large and remote areas. Their policy narrative, however, tapped into the then Government's wish to minimise the fallout as it shifted people off Community Development Employment Projects into mainstream welfare and jobs. Meeting the Government's priority of Indigenous job numbers gave the program breathing space to document the less obvious environmental (and indeed health) benefits.

A negative example of blurred objectives was Home Insulation, where the job-creation urgencies distorted and overrode the environmental objectives. Hence, the early program termination and the high number of failure nominations from interviewees.

Similarly, the interviewees agreed that evidence-based policymaking (EBPM) would improve the prospects of Cabinet endorsement and successful implementation. Once again, the exigencies of environmental policy saw them modify the principles of EBPM to suit the matter at hand.

Even in a matter as important as the Murray Darling Basin, one interviewee remarked that 100 years of inaction or non-cooperation had produced "20 or 30 years clear evidence" of over-allocation of water. Yet it was only the political "ten-year drought" crisis that had finally triggered policy action.

Other cases provide contrasting evidence on EBPM in environment policy. Working on Country was rated successful, although its thin evidence base only improved gradually over time. Similarly, its successful precursor, Indigenous Protected Areas, used accessible and self-reported measures for Indigenous disadvantage, rather than trying to capture elusive and costly-to-measure biodiversity outcomes.

Conversely, a surfeit of 'evidence' was not necessarily a good thing for positive program outcomes. For example, the exhaustive data-first scientific evidence gathering in the early phases of Regional Forest Agreements and Marine Protected Areas became paralysing. These masses of evidence, moreover, were not enough to prevent abrupt or politically based policy decisions, based on expediency as much as ecology. Both these programs attracted mixed success-failure ratings from interviewees.

The apparent EBPM contradictions may be explained as follows. To be sure, environment policy benefits from robust data sets, of which many are available. However, officials were loath to jeopardise transient policy opportunities for want of presenting comprehensive data, which in any case might not be absorbed by ministers, or might clog up political timelines. Several interviewees owned up to a pragmatic approach of quickly scanning for and collating information within a brief 'new policy' timeframe. Such information might support what they intuited to be good public policy, but it did not necessarily amount to hard quantitative evidence.

Interviewees mentioned other success factors that are highly profiled (see Table 2.2) in the literature – adequacy of resources, policy origins, and policy design – but fewer than ten endorsed any one of these factors as a critical driver of success.

Rather than emphasising the need for adequate resources, most interviewees saw scarce resources as a commonplace, and not necessarily a hindrance.

For example, the tacit approach in Marine Protected Areas was to get the MPA system declared, and then try to boost the resources later on. Similarly, when Government failed to make routine financial allocations for administering the *EPBC Act*, this may have been a blessing in disguise, as it forced the department to hone the relevant skills in house.

Counter-intuitively, a surfeit of resources could stifle program success. The large and sudden windfall for Home Insulation became one factor that increased the chances of the eventual program failure. In addition, as one interviewee noted, liberal environmental funding can be used to buy off dissenting States or vested interests, rather than necessarily securing the best policy. This idea, that generous resources could actually impede policy success, is rarely found in the literature.

In contrast with the Chapter 2 literature on policy agenda setting, only five interviewees thought that the policy origins were a significant indicator of the prospects for policy success. From their inside vantage point, most interviewees perceived 'policy origins' to be varied and diffuse, rather than logical or predictive. These origins might involve moments of crisis, covert deal making, or sheer luck.

For example, only the millennium drought triggered a step change in water policy, while Home Insulation was an offshoot of an unprecedented global financial crisis. The large Biodiversity Fund created in 2011 was, more than anything else, a political trade-off to secure passage of the carbon tax legislation. Indeed, one seasoned official who was interviewed at the time predicted correctly that the Fund would soon be offered up in savings.

As it has happened, significant federal environment policy of recent years has also arisen from election commitments, the environment minister or his office, the main opposition party, narrowly based external lobbying, international commitments, or ongoing departmental work.

Interviewees endorsed early engagement in design parameters, and calibrating the scale of response to the size of the problem, but only nine (see Table 4.1) rated attention to program design as a significant shaper of policy success. They were more concerned with adapting the design as economic and political ramifications unfolded during the implementation, rather than trying to get the design spot-on at the policy proposal stage. They also noted that there could be scope to influence program design in the lead up to a Cabinet Decision, or indeed if the Decision itself left the design parameters open.

Home Insulation and the Natural Heritage Trust were cited as examples of questionable and difficult-to-implement policy designs being locked in too early, because of political imperatives and stakeholder demands. On the other hand, the lengthy design period available for Green Loans was nullified by the Department's poor-quality oversight, with an extended failure to get a ministerial sign-off on the program design.

4.2 Novel predictors: policy mandate and policy agency

Significant numbers of interviewees nominated factors that are less well studied in the literature – the degree of the policy mandate and the degree of policy agency exercised by officials – as predictors of policy success.

Nearly half of the interviewees thought that environment policy had a better chance of success when the Commonwealth had a strong mandate, be that political, legislative, or brokered with the States.

Federal protection of terrestrial and marine biodiversity, they noted, was elusive until such time as the Commonwealth acquired useful program and policy levers through the Natural Heritage Trust and the *EPBC Act 1999*. Even after this enactment, the States wouldn't necessarily "accept the legitimacy" of the Commonwealth environmental role, as they regarded land and water management as their issues. Tactically, the Commonwealth could try to bypass the States, if they were reluctant policy partners, or it could "work with the States" in cases where the States held the constitutional remit and the expertise, or controlled the delivery mechanisms.

A capable minister with Cabinet clout, they added, could get more mileage out of a mandate. Labor Environment Minister (1988-90, and briefly in 1994) Richardson and Liberal Environment Minister (1996-2001) Hill were singled out by half of the 17 interviewees who mentioned this ministerial factor. While the former made tactical environmental determinations with an eye to political leverage in key seats, the latter sought systemic change in environmental management.

Discounting the party politics of the Government as a predictor of environment policy success, inter-viewees stressed instead the value of bipartisan support. Policies that survived changes of government included the forests and oceans policies of pre-March 1996, and Working on Country of pre-December 2007.

Over half of the interviewees represented their environment policy roles more as avoiding failure than pursuing success, as an attempt to avoid further loss of environmental values or at least to 'hold the line' environmentally.

Nevertheless, a deeper analysis of the interview transcripts and case studies revealed the exercise of 'policy agency' as an instrumental factor for policy success. Again, 'agency' is defined here as the self-directed actions of officials to use policy to achieve a particular result for the good of the environ-ment. All but five transcripts evidenced such 'agency' behaviours, although few interviewees would be inclined to voice that actual term to describe what they did or what they observed.

It is not unreasonable to express scepticism about officials emphasising the importance of official agency. As the ironic expression goes, they would say that, wouldn't they? However, the detail of the interview transcripts did not support the idea that officials saw themselves as all-important. If anything, the interviewees were diffident about programs that had had their direct input, tending to illuminate failures rather than boast of success. And, once again, the overall reasonableness of their assessments of program success or failure is given credence by its correspondence with assessments (Table 3.2) derived by using the Marsh and McConnell Framework.

The main clue to 'agency' behaviour was the interviewees' recurrent references to them or their colleagues continually probing for openings to get policy ideas on to the Government's agenda. Though such policy openings were known to be rare and unpredictable, interviewees commonly reported nurturing policy seeds over long timeframes, and keeping policy ideas and costings at the ready. These seeds might be inserted into the process whenever the Departmental Executive or Minister looked to be receptive; when election statements or political negotiations created opportunities; when policies could be aligned with emerging and larger strategies; or when proposals could absorb budget under-spends or enhance budget bids.

Not everybody, so the interviewees clarified, excelled at exploiting these transient policy openings. Three interviewees commented that fewer officials did the real policymaking than lay people would ever realise. Such individuals were the policy "inside runners". Only "certain individuals" had the strategic abilities or could ask the right questions to achieve policy "rigour and discipline".

One interviewee thought this "intrinsic" policy flair was not readily teachable because "some people never get policy". Neither would it follow that the most effective policy activists would be the high-ranking SES officers, although some were. But this type of higher-level policy acumen, it is to be noted, bears comparison with sought-after capabilities in the SES selection criteria.

4.3 How do officials exercise their policy agency?

Several strategies recurred in the exercise of policy agency. The environment officials were extremely patient at sowing policy seeds. They built up a deep understanding of stakeholder positions, so that they could think beyond the Canberra 'bubble' and overcome opposition to promising new policies. They had no qualms about linking environment policy to broader social or economic agendas. Finally, if their intuitions favoured a certain policy course, they were not fazed by inconclusive evidence.

In a number of the interview transcripts, there were convincing examples of policy agency, creative in execution, yet based on hard-won bureaucratic know how.

When the Natural Heritage Trust Commonwealth-State Agreements were being negotiated over 2002-04, a senior official advocated clauses barring land clearing in the States, seeing this as a strategic win in an otherwise cumbersome model. Another senior official realised that certain *EPBC Act 1999* provisions could be invoked to progress the stalled Marine Protected Areas agenda, through bioregional plans.

Similarly, the Working on Country officials capitalised on a happenstance convergence of interests. They craved environmental funding for the Indigenous estate, while Indigenous people wanted wages and respect for land management, and Government was eager to move Indigenous people off a lapsing 'welfare' program into employment. The officials engineered an unusual delegation of authority, from the Minister to the Secretary, and this sped up the approval of the first 10 projects.

Conversely, programs could be crippled by an absence of 'agency'. Fearing the worst for the Home Insulation Program, three interviewees flagged the risks (to senior managers in the Environment or Prime Minister's Department or to ministerial offices) then literally absented themselves, by quietly moving jobs. Those officials who remained to implement the program committed 'agency by omission'. They failed to attach the Risk Register to a critical April 2009 brief for Minister Garrett (Australian Royal Commission into the Home Insulation Program 2014b, 531). They otherwise provided (as one interviewee put it) "sterile" or less-than-frank briefings on the critical safety and fraud issues that were emerging.

As another example, the Green Loans program suffered from poor staffing decisions and inadequate management oversight, as Departmental attention was diverted to the large and high profile Home Insulation Program. The Department wasn't "frank with the Government about the risks" in Green Loans.

The exercise of policy agency that is under discussion here would rarely be evident to the external observer. Such activism was characterised by interviewees as "covert" or hidden "in the DNA of the organisation". Officials tended not to discuss it with each other.

One of the underlying factors sparking agency behaviour was that interviewees did not expect to experience a neat 'policy cycle', such as is set out in some public policy texts. With rare exceptions, their policy work did not proceed neatly from first principles through to optimal solutions. It was more like being inserted in the middle of an intractable issue, where significant concessions might have been made already:

> 'You don't so much go in a policy cycle but take actions and see attempts to derail the policy. You see the lines drawn in the sand. You can get derailed; go backwards and backwards again, and then try for another round. So you bounce back and forth, until you break through.'

The contested and unruly nature of environmental policy problems helps to explain why the officials might exercise forms of 'agency'. They might proceed through veiled manoeuvres, massaging the policy objectives, corralling the stakeholders, and working around the evidence gaps.

Finally, their 'agency' also stemmed from an alignment between the Departmental objectives and their values as officials. They said that they joined the Department "for the work" to collaborate with "people who are genuinely committed".

The interviewees all regarded the judicious exercise of agency as a legitimate and healthy aspect of new-policy formulation. Governments, they argued, depend on and expect policy advice, much of which is "devised and crafted" or "crafted and fine-tuned" inside the public service. As a Tier 1 put it:

> 'I don't have this view that the role of the APS is just to apply the policies of the Government of the day. The APS is highly skilled, highly intelligent, highly experienced, and I happen to believe, and not just in the environment area but in a whole host of areas, that a large amount of policy comes out of the APS or is crafted and fine-tuned by the APS. So the Department should always be conscious of the political side of the equation...'

Such an exercise of agency exceeds the roles that are usually ascribed to officials in the policy literature, or indeed in the conventional public service policy guides like the *Better Practice Guide* (Australian National Audit Office, 2006). But this softening of the traditional 'Westminster' approach is acknowledged in the reform blueprint *Ahead of the Game* (Advisory Group on Reform of Australian Government Administration, 2010). The blueprint confirms that ministers make the final decisions but allows they "work in partnership" with the public service to "develop and implement".

Similarly, Stephen Sedgwick as Australian Public Service Commissioner argued (Towell, 2013) for a more engaged public service with "strategic foresight capability". As the head of ANZSOG, Banks (2013, 4) opined that policy officials ought to find the right balance between respecting the decisions of Government and doing a "solid job in advising and informing government policy decisions".

In summary, although the policy officials interviewed revealed a surprisingly high degree of agency, their underlying intent was to deliver better public policy. Many had elected to work in the Environment Department because the portfolio function aligned with their personal values.

For all that, instances in this study of leaking confidential documents (e.g. as occurred in the Regional Forest Agreements process) or improper behaviour (e.g. as exhibited by the rogue Tier 3 or Executive Level 2 in the Green Loans Program) underscore that 'agency' behaviour can easily move from being appropriate to quite inappropriate, to the extent of contravening the APS Code of Conduct and the *Public Service Act 1999.*

Parallel examples of inappropriate agency behaviour are evident in other high-profile policy debacles that took place over the study period, such as the Australian Wheat Board scandal and the Children Overboard incident.

With agency, then, comes responsibility. As one interviewee argued, where policy failure does occur (provided that the responsibility for failure can be attributed), then the public servants should be held to account.

Chapter 5

Case Studies of Success or Failure in Environment Policy

Revisiting the policy literature and the interview findings, this chapter examines in detail reasons for the relative success of two important federal environment policies (Fuel Quality Standards and Working on Country) as against the disappointments of two others (Home Insulation Program and Sustainable Population Strategy).

The two successful policies both rated well with interviewees, and also under the application of the process, program and political dimensions in the Marsh and McConnell Framework. In other respects, they are a study in contrasts.

Fuel Quality was a rare case where environmental policy started from 'first principles' and ticked the boxes for successful policy development, those that are emphasised in the literature. In the case of Working on Country, the core environmental objectives travelled somewhat under disguise, and there was limited upfront evidence for the distinctive policy design. Fuel Quality got an unexpected fillip from minority-party political trades of the time, whereas in the case of Working on Country, tactical policy officials rode the mainstream political agenda, which was to get Indigenous people off welfare and into jobs. If the proof is in the pudding, both these programs have succeeded and grown over a decade or more.

The Home Insulation Program rated very poorly with interviewees. Neither it nor the Sustainable Population Strategy is flattered by application of the Marsh and McConnell Framework. In their different ways, both programs illustrate the pitfalls of top-down or politically driven policy, where the objective evidence is not to the fore and the influence or advice of top Departmental officials is stifled.

In the case of Home Insulation, the Environment officials did originally propose a more robust program model. This was overridden by a risky and impracticable design dictated by the economic stimulus demands of the Global Financial Crisis. Once the Department had absorbed that setback, it did not acquit itself with great distinction, as the program unravelled. On the other hand, the trajectory of the Sustainable Population Strategy was diverted at the outset by a Ministerial insistence on what the priorities ought to be. While the Environment Department nominally had carriage of the Strategy, in effect the central agencies (Treasury and the Prime Minister's Department) dominated policy developments. The 'solutions' in the Strategy bore little relationship to the 'issues' and they sidelined the available evidence.

Neither of these two programs has proven durable. After beginning with a fanfare in 2009, Home Insulation was abruptly terminated in 2010. The diversionary suburban, regional and roads measures that were announced in 2011 for the Population Strategy petered out, leaving little lasting or coherent impact.

5.1 More successful policy: Fuel Quality Standards

The *Fuel Quality Standards Act 2000* is a rare example of environmental policy work that started almost from 'first principles' and not in a chaotic or contested middle game. Aided by a touch of luck, it proceeded through largely evidence-based policy formulation towards a 'win-win' outcome for the environment and the economy.

In tune with the 'preconditions for success' at Chapter 2, the solutions (better fuel standards) were practicable and enforceable. They followed logically from the policy issues at hand (poor fuel and vehicle standards, that were perpetuating pollution, and lowering industry and health standards). The original policy 'template' of 2000-2002 has proved useful and durable, its imprint still visible in policies of a decade later.

Of the 51 Environment Department interviewees, eight commented on this policy. All rated it successful, and none rated it as failed. A similar number made a more general point, that this kind of 'brown' or pollution-abatement program more often succeeds than the typical 'green' or biodiversity-enhancement program. Assessed against the Marsh and McConnell Framework, Fuel Quality Standards impresses on the process, programmatic and political dimensions. If anything, the Government of the time underplayed the success story.

Fuel Quality Standards: Description

While Fuel Quality may be touted as sound policy with logical origins and objectives, it also got unexpected fillips, from the politics of the time and from sheer luck.

The Department had been patiently developing the case for cleaner fuels over a period, but without any political traction. Critically, its background work underpinned the National Environment Protection Measure for Ambient Air Quality set in 1998 by the National [Commonwealth-State] Environment Protection Council. This Measure (Environment Australia, 2000, 3) was a framework of national standards and goals for "six most significant" air pollutants – for which motor vehicle fuel emissions were a major source. These six were CO, NO2, SO2, lead, ozone, and particulate matter.

Fuel Quality vaulted onto the agenda when, unbeknownst to the Department, the Democrats insisted on its inclusion in the Measures for a Better Environment (MBE) package. Trading with the Democrats to get his GST legislation passed in the Senate, Prime Minister Howard agreed to this package of $400 million over the four years 2000–2004. The MBE was developed over just a few days. As one interviewee put it, the overall quality suffered accordingly:

> 'I would see as not good policy the sort of stuff we had to do for the [Democrats] in the MBE. Some of the ideas, such as Fuel Quality Standards, were quite good but we ended up with far too much money to be able to spend it properly.'

The background to the 'too much money' is startling. Hartcher (2011) reported, and this research confirmed (Costello, 1 November 2013), that Howard took Treasurer Costello's aside to offer the Democrats '400' to mean $400 million rather than $400,000 as intended. The unplanned largesse helped pave the way for the Fuel Quality legislation of 2000 and its ensuing fuel standards.

The objectives of the Act are to reduce the level of pollutants and emissions arising from the use of fuel that may cause environmental and health problems; facilitate the adoption of better engine and emission control technology; allow the more effective operation of engines; and ensure consumers get appropriate information about fuel.

Attending the development of the legislation was a suite of four discussion papers (see Department of the Environment, 2015a) and a Summary Report (Environment Australia, 2000). Determinations and Regulations made under the Act enabled the first national fuel standards to come into play in January 2002. The historic change at the bowser for motorists was the banning forthwith of leaded petrol. The first set of standards also lowered the permissible level of sulphur in diesel fuel.

Since 2002, there has been a regular program of policy refinement and review. New Determinations were issued for Autogas, Biodiesel, Ethanol, and Ethanol 85, over 2003-2012 (Department of the Environment, 2015a). The first Review of the Act in 2005 concluded that its objectives were sound and generally being met, but recommended improvements in complementary State legislation, fuel sampling, emergency provisions, approval procedures, and stakeholder communication. A second and broader review of the Act's contemporary appropriateness and relevance began in 2015 (Marsden Jacob Associates, 2015).

Fuel Quality Standards: Results

Two interviewees claimed that Fuel Quality was the most successful, but ironically the least visible, environment program they had ever been associated with. One referred to it as 'close to invisible' despite the 'more efficient/less polluting' vehicles that it allowed to enter the Australian vehicle fleet. The other also referred to the cleaner vehicle fleet, and the attractive cost-benefit ratio that had sold the policy to Treasury and to Government:

> 'The biggest policy success delivered by the Department in terms of objective outcomes was the fuels program. It leveraged enormous positive outcomes both in health/well being and air quality. It provided benefits in hard numbers for a really tiny injection of hard cash, most of which came because we were able to work with Treasury (to calculate the monetary benefits of avoided health costs compared to the cost to industry to improve the quality of fuel)…The program has had positive spin-offs that will be felt for years. It is possibly not mentioned often as a successful environment program as it was a very technical program and people are often thrown by technical details…The Government didn't realise the good success story.'

These and other interviewees remarked that often the policy rationale for a 'brown' or pollution-abatement agenda such as fuel quality could be articulated clearly and justified on cost-benefit grounds. They compared this to the 'green' agenda, where often it was difficult to design cost-effective biodiversity policies with clear objectives that logically linked the issue and the outcome.

Indeed, the initial 2002 standards for petrol and diesel were put into effect with few difficulties, as were subsequent standards for other fuel types.

The Act began with a clearly articulated monitoring, compliance and enforcement program, and this too has carried forward (Department of the Environment, 2015a).

Fuel suppliers must keep a document trail and provide it on request. From 2003, fuel producers and importers were required to report annually to the Department. The Department accredits under the Act the inspectors and sample testers who carry out the inspection program of importers, refiners, distributors and service stations. In a recent review (Hart Energy, 2014), Australia's fuel quality monitoring regime appeared to compare reasonably well with those of other nations. Only about 1.3 per cent of 5,275 samples taken over 2011-2013 were non-compliant.

Concentrating on its initial 1998-2002 phase, Fuel Quality also gets a good health check, according to the dimensions of the Marsh and McConnell Framework.

The process dimension was thorough, beginning with the Commonwealth-State agreement to the underpinning air quality framework. The main consultation phase (Environment Australia, 2001) was open enough to draw in the range of opinions from governments, the fuel and car industries, and technical experts. The Act set up a Consultative Committee comprising these players, plus environmental and consumer representatives.

Similarly, the program dimension showed good results. Although Australia had been slow (six years behind the US) to ban leaded petrol, once it did so this was well handled. As noted, the subsequent train of Determinations for other fuels was also implemented smoothly. Although Australia is not a world leader in actual fuel standards, its monitoring and inspection regime has been credible and looks comparable to international practice. The effects were achieved with an efficient use of resources. While industry had to adjust, there were not adverse impacts on equity.

The political dimension was a considerable success, in the sense that potentially hard-to-follow or unpopular technical reforms were stepped through, with no major negative fallout to the Howard Government of the day. On the contrary, interviewees thought the Government rather neglected to claim the positive political credits due.

Fuel Quality Standards: Drivers of Success

Conventional factors for policy success that are drummed in within the policy literature – soundness of origins, clear objectives, evidence, design, and consultation – made near-textbook appearances here.

To begin with, this rather technical new policy had in its origins a clear (economic) driver that made sense and could be explained simply, as this interviewee put it:

'The fuels policy had a clear driver. Australia was becoming an island of dirty fuel and we would be faced with importing fuel. Before the change to fuel standards we couldn't bring efficient cars or trucks in because of the low quality fuel.'

The portfolio of evidence for the policy was strong. The debilitating health effects of lead exposure were long established. The Air Quality Measure of 1998 set a framework for control of lead and other "most significant" ambient air pollutants. There was strong evidence that quick economic and industry gains would come from better fuel quality, leaving elbowroom to measure the air-quality and health impacts over a longer period. Consultation took place with key interest groups, and was open and well managed. The fuel pollution, vehicle technology, and health, objectives of the policy were clearly stated, and found reasonable expression in the legislation.

In what never became a highly politicised process, the 'agency' of the Environment officials was exerted more in the backroom. The game-breakers, such as they were, came through luck and political circumstance rather than masterstrokes by officials. But the corporate skills of certain key officials interviewed for this book made a big difference, combining as they did uncommon technical knowledge and policy savvy. When their 'luck' arrived, these officials had kept the evidence in reach to exploit it.

Fuel Quality Standards: Postscript

There is substantial evidence of useful longer-term impacts arising from the Fuel Quality policy.

The national *State of the Air Report* (Department of Sustainability Environment Water Population and Communities, 2011b) confirmed that by 2008 the policy had driven significant decreases in four of the targeted air pollutants:

"CO, NO2, SO2 and lead levels have all declined in urban air to levels significantly below the national air quality standards. The air quality rating for all these pollutants is Good or Very Good in most regions. *These improvements are largely because of better standards for fuel quality and motor vehicle emissions.* [author emphasis] Ozone and particulate matter levels did not decrease in the assessment period."

Despite these air quality improvements, it was not yet confirmed that the large 'avoided health costs' claimed at the outset had been realised. The National Environmental Protection Council (2011, 28) still found "significant health effects at current levels of air pollution in Australian cities" and recommended stricter air-pollution standards.

The Hart Energy (2014) report suggested tightening the existing specifications for gasoline (petrol), diesel, biodiesel and E85 fuel. Aligning with lower European Union sulphur limits in petrol, it argued, could "enable advanced emission controls" for Australian vehicles. The Climate Change Authority (2014) said that Australia's light vehicle emissions efficiency was improving but still lagged behind many countries. It recommended halving the average CO_2 (not CO) emissions per kilometre of the light vehicle fleet by 2025. With action not forthcoming, the CCA concern became an issue (Ferraro, 13 July 2017) again in mid 2017.

Against all this, the 2015 Review of the Act (Marsden Jacob Associates, 2015) said that "all" regulatory options were on the table: government regulation, co-regulation, voluntary standards, or no standards. The then current (government regulation) regime did include elements of co-regulation, with fuel suppliers, producers and importers. In the event, despite Australia's generous fuel sulphur allowance, the 2016 report of the 2015 review (Marsden Jacobs Associates, 2016) reconfirmed the Act's continuing relevance and effectiveness, and found that its health benefits considerably exceeded the implementation costs.

5.2 More successful policy: Working on Country

Among the 51 interviewees for this study, 23 referred to Working on Country as a rare environmental program success. None considered it a failure. This section describes the origins of the program and its successes since 2007. These successes are validated against the Marsh and McConnell Framework. The keys to success, according to interviewees, were the lengthy 'road testing' of the program concept, authentic stakeholder engagement, and subsuming the environment objectives into economic and social objectives. Providing fair wages and on-costs for the on-country rangers may not sound like a revolutionary advance, but in this context it was a decisive break from orthodoxy. In contrast with Home Insulation, senior environment officials held sway over the policy development, and they used the political narrative to their advantage rather than being overwhelmed by it.

Working on Country: Description

A small group of academic researchers and Indigenous leaders had long promoted the benefits of better support for Indigenous rangers, and for Indigenous aspirations to care for country. The small-but-successful Contract Employment Program for Aboriginals in Natural and Cultural Resource Management (CEPANCRM) and Indigenous Protected Areas (IPA) programs had led the way for attempts to introduce wages for Indigenous land management. Both these programs capitalised on customary Indigenous practices.

The federal government announced Working on Country in May 2007 with funding of $47.6m over four years (Department of the Environment and Water Resources, 2007). This was embedded in a larger initiative to transition Indigenous people from Community Development Employment Projects (CDEP) into paid employment (ANAO, 2011).

In formal terms, the first program objective was to give Indigenous people the means to undertake environmental work that met their 'caring for country' aspirations and the Australian Government's environmental responsibilities. The second objective was to provide a mechanism for Indigenous people, including CDEP participants, to move into jobs. This second rationale was what got the program traction inside the Government.

Working on Country began as a small 'bespoke' program. Table 5.1 shows its rapid growth, highly unusual for a land management and biodiversity program.

Table 5.1: Working on Country, funding tranches and job levels, 2007–2012

Date	Policy driver	Program funding	Jobs
May 2007	Community Development Employment Projects reforms	$47.6m over 4 years for positions across Australia	100
Sept 2007	In June 2007, the Howard Government announced the phased removal of CDEP, in the NT Emergency Response to address child sexual abuse as reported by Anderson and Wild (2007).	$63.7m over 3 years for positions in the NT	169
Dec 2007	Rudd election commitment, as part of the new 'Caring for our Country'.	$90m over 5 years building on the original May 2007 decision	200
Nov 2008	COAG National Agreement on Indigenous Reform in Economic Participation – abolition of CDEP in regional areas from 1 July 2009 – for ranger positions on non-Indigenous tenure; mature age and trainee positions	$64.3m over 5 years – Comprising $42.5m for 100 positions (regional), $15.6m for 60 positions (casual), and $6.2m for 32 (initially 50) traineeships	192
May 2010	CDEP reforms in the Torres Strait	$9.2m over 5 years in the Torres Strait	21
Feb 2012	'Stronger Futures' Package as part of the second phase of the NT Emergency Response under the Gillard Government	$23.3m over 4 years in the NT	50
Total		**$298.1m over 5 years**	**732**

Key sources: Environment Department Annual Reports of 2007-08 to 2012-13.

By November 2013, the program employed over 690 rangers out of 732 positions funded, in more than 90 projects, primarily in desert or coastal areas of remote and regional Australia (Department of Sustainability Environment Water Population and Communities, 2013, p. 24). At May 2013, the majority of the projects were in the Northern Territory (33) and Queensland (30) with 18 in northern and central Western Australia. There were ten in South Australia and only nine in other states, New South Wales (5), Victoria (2) and Tasmania (2) (Department of the Environment, 2013b).

Working on Country: Results

Program success is well documented, in environment, employment, and social terms.

Illustration 5.1: Kija Rangers (WA) on Gouldian Finch survey, 2017

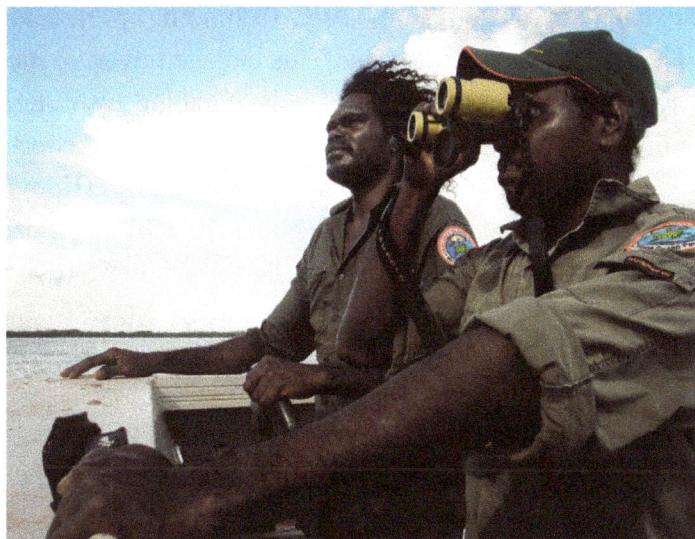

Source: John Skuja, for Kija Rangers, Kimberley Land Council

Government and external reviews have established that Working on Country met its stated objectives and delivered on a broader range of economic, social and health outcomes (Allen Consulting Group, 2011; ANAO, 2011; Caring for our Country Review Team, 2012; Department of Sustainability Environment Water Population and Communities, 2011a; Smyth, 2011a; Smyth, 2011b; Urbis, 2012; WalterTurnbull, 2010).

The Department of Finance and Deregulation's confidential Strategic Review of Indigenous Expenditure (2010) concluded that ranger programs such as Working on Country provide "'real jobs' that have effective environmental outcomes, are sustainable and create meaningful and ongoing employment pathways".

In 2013, the Environment Department adjudged the program as a successful cross-cultural model achieving environmental outcomes benefiting Australia. All the projects were managing matters of National Environmental Significance under the *EPBC Act* and 91 per cent managed 'key threatening processes' such as feral pigs, cats, marine debris, and invasive grasses. Over 91 per cent helped to protect threatened fauna species. Some 71 per cent were tackling weeds of national significance, while 77 per cent were managing culturally significant sites. Most of the projects supported the transfer of Indigenous cultural knowledge, including customary early dry-season patch burning as a fire management tool (Department of Sustainability Environment Water Population and Communities, June 2013).

Although the cumulative environmental effects remain untested, environmental success is evident in individual projects. One example is a $2.3m (total 2012-13 funding) project to sustain the Martu communities of the Western Desert in Western Australia. This engaged over 90 men in three communities, contributing to the removal of nearly 24,000 feral camels, cleaning up waterholes, monitoring fauna such as bilby and rock wallaby, practising traditional fire management to reduce wildfire risk, removing buffel grass infestations, and managing Canning Stock Route tourism. (Kanyirninpa Jukurrpa, 2013). Environmental outcomes in other parts of Australia include the Dhimurru project, controlling 'crazy ants', and the Ngurrara rangers, who found the elusive desert spade-foot frog during climate-change monitoring. In 2017, Kimberley Bardi Jawi rangers (ABC News, 5 May 2017) made the first-ever verified observations of the Nicobar pigeon on Australian soil.

The employment outcomes of the program stand out, with a job retention rate of approximately 80 per cent over 12 months for the 690 rangers employed by 2013. In addition, 76 per cent participated in accredited conservation and land management training (Department of Sustainability Environment Water Population and Communities, 2012). High rates of retention and training enabled 5-10 per cent of the rangers leaving the program each year to get jobs in mining and other sectors (Department of Sustainability Environment Water Population and Communities, June 2013, p. 15).

Research demonstrates savings, through reduced welfare payments as unemployed people move into jobs, and through increased tax contributions by project employees (Department of Sustainability Environment Water Population and Communities, 2012). A 2011 estimate was that these savings deflated the program's true cost as much as 23 per cent below the budget cost (Allen Consulting Group, 2011). Later research (Social Ventures Australia, 2014) suggests about a $3 benefit in social and economic terms for every dollar invested with the Martu Working on Country programs. Studies of Indigenous ranger work have produced statistical evidence of medical benefits (Burgess et al., 2009; Garnett and Sithole, 2007;

Urbis, 2012). The Burgess study found caring-for-country work was significantly associated with more exercise and bush-food consumption, boosting health on clinical indicators such as blood pressure, diabetes rates, and cardiovascular disease risks. In short, economic analyses establish benefits in terms of avoided health and welfare costs that probably match or exceed the budgetary cost of the program.

Working on Country also appears successful, with few negatives, when it is re-examined in Marsh and McConnell terms.

The process was notable for its sound Budget and Cabinet execution, balance between government and Indigenous interests, flexible guidelines, adequate resources, and positive early (by 2010) evaluations. The main potential negative of the process was the risks arising from the high pressure it placed on Indigenous governance capacities.

The program met its job and environment objectives each year, succeeded over a seven-year run, target-ed significant environmental problems, sustained high rates of job retention and follow-up employment, and spun off health and welfare gains that effectively reduced the cost to budget. While the program's 'high' budget cost was perceived early on as a distinct aberration or a negative, this concern was neu-tralised by the later gains. Clearly, the program used its 'high' cost to target particular 'actors or inter-ests', the Indigenous communities. But these were disadvantaged interests, that had unique skill sets to make the program a success, and previous 'low' cost approaches had not worked.

Politically, Working on Country had bipartisan support, gave ministers a ready success story, contribut-ed to the 'Closing the Gap' employment targets, and was esteemed by Indigenous communities.

Working on Country: Drivers of Success

The success of the Working on Country environmental program over more than seven years and through three changes of government is notable. The program succeeded in remote-area Indigenous policy where many programs fail. Why was this so?

Some conventional factors for policy success in the literature – good design and sound consultation – were put in place. While the literature calls for clear objectives and clear evidence, in this particular case it made good tactical sense to blur the 'primary' environmental objectives in favour of employment ob-jectives, for which the evidence was easier to collect initially. The active 'agency' exerted by committed and knowledgeable officials was a key factor.

The long gestation period partly explains the program's success. Its seed was the caring for country work in the Northern and Central Land Councils, where Indigenous rangers had long argued for fair wages. The concept was closely modelled on CEPANCRM, though that boutique program had only ever spent $25 million, on a few weeks' work for each of its 8,490 participants. Meanwhile, Mabo and subsequent decisions, while paving the way for over 30 per cent of Australian land to fall under Indigenous tenure (Altman & Markham, 2013), had prompted the invention of Indigenous Protected Areas in 1996. About half the Working on Country projects sat inside IPAs, but the new program achieved something IPAs couldn't – payment of award wages.

Tuning in to genuine government interest, the Environment Department had drafted a new policy proposal for its 2007–2008 Budget Portfolio Submission. The then Departmental Secretary had taken the head of Treasury 'on country' to see ranger work. The latter repaid the favour by backing the proposal in Canberra discussions. Having a rare opportunity, the officials went for early winners over program purity, favouring areas with sound Indigenous governance:

> 'We went for success. We had several discussions about how this isn't about equity. We picked winners because if we fail it will be another 10–15 years before it would be tried again.'

Working on Country also traded on the generally bipartisan support for credible programs designed to address Indigenous unemployment. Like the IPA program, it survived changes of the federal government. Working on Country was initiated by Liberal Government and yet continued by a Labor Government six months later.

The incentive levels, which were a distinct policy shift, were instrumental in the successful program rollout. If full time, rangers could earn about $30,000 annually as trainees, rising to $65,000 for senior rangers. Wage rates were set by contracting organisations and aligned with relevant awards. Before Working on Country, ranger groups had relied for income on CDEP, only about $12,000 a head annually.

Counting overheads, each ranger position would cost about $100,000 all up, a high unit cost for such a program. As one would expect, the Finance Department challenged this in the early negotiations, and the Environment Minister feared it as an exposure point. If, however, the rangers' work was 'real', it follows that they had a real case for a fair wage. Secondly, perhaps this 'point of difference' helps to explain the lasting success in a notoriously difficult policy space. And, as noted, evidence began to accrue that the 'high' costs to budget were in any event offset to a degree by health and welfare savings.

From prototype through to implementation, the program was characterised by genuine stakeholder engagement. The Environment Department brought in Indigenous stakeholders from around the country. Experienced project staffers were not afraid to trek out to communities to see what was possible:

'Working on Country worked because, first of all having an understanding of what country means to people and secondly, having again the networks, the relationships and being prepared to be in the communities. Taking the call when someone says "I want to talk to you about the program" and getting yourself on a plane and then driving yourself west of wherever you land and meeting with a group of people you have never met in your life and talking with them.'

Once senior officials realised that their proposal had a real chance in the 2007-08 budget, they got design input from experienced departmental hands and spoke in confidence with Aboriginal leaders. The consultations soothed Aboriginal concerns about Canberra's bona fides, and Canberra's concerns about the process for filling ranger jobs. It turned out that the funded communities agreed which men and women were respected as CDEP rangers and had the best claims to Working on Country jobs.

Like CEPANCRM and IPAs, Working on Country deliberately employed dual or 'blurred' objectives. The byword was to emphasise the government agenda on Indigenous welfare, rather than directly pushing the environment values. This shakes the conventional theory that clarity in policy objectives, with a demonstrable link between rationale and solution, is the ultimate precursor to program success.

The dualistic program objectives, if tricky in terms of portfolio accountability, made a lot of sense from an Indigenous perspective. They also allowed the Department to demonstrate job outcomes quickly, all the while buying time to build up the social and environmental cases. As noted above, evidence on social and health benefits has accumulated since 2007, while there are also environmental successes.

Working on Country had four critical design features that enabled much quicker implementation than most environment programs: These were sound governance, modest scale, ongoing funding, and an unusual delegation of authority.

The program's scale was modest, only 100 ranger jobs in the first year. Existing Land Councils and other Indigenous bodies provided the governance structures, and a ready supply of proven Indigenous rangers to fill funded positions. The first projects all took place on Indigenous tenures, although this requirement was relaxed in 2008. Funding was 'ongoing' rather than 'lapsing' (that is, requiring re-submission after four years). Finally, the Minister agreed to delegate his expensing authority to the Secretary and his deputies, speeding up approvals and reducing the risk of under-spends.

Importantly, the Departmental Executive got the design right, both for the government and for the funded organisations. The guidelines accepted Indigenous understandings of land and were calibrated to suit local needs. The incentives were high enough to win engagement but not so high as to invite 'rorting'. The program had to be delivered and staffed by Indigenous organisations, which reduced the employment risks for government, but gave the organisations a strong sense of responsibility about the on-the-job performance of their rangers.

Research since 2007 (Allen Consulting Group, 2011; Putnis et al., 2007; Smyth, 2011b; Urbis, 2012; WalterTurnbull, 2010) has confirmed the contribution of the design factors. The first rounds of the program were implemented very quickly, as the applicants held tenure to the land and the program had the support of traditional landowners. Flexible funding and governance arrangements empowered Indigenous communities to manage natural and cultural values of land and sea according to their own aspirations. The payment of award wages up-valued customary knowledge. The program's extension to non-Indigenous land tenure in 2008 paved the way for participation in the southern States. Finally, there was enough funding to cover field coordinators (often non-Indigenous) for the ranger groups, and also proper equipment and training for project viability.

Working on Country: Postscript

It's important to keep the success story in perspective. Working on Country at no stage represented as much as 5 per cent of annual Commonwealth expenditures on Indigenous programs. Its past successes were no guarantee for its future.

The 2013 shift of the program from the Environment Department into the Prime Minister's portfolio severed the direct and fruitful link between Indigenous caring for country aspirations and the biodiversity objectives of the Environment Department.

A year later, in the rationalisation of Indigenous programs into five broad streams, the program was folded into a larger Indigenous employment program and later into the overall Indigenous Advancement Strategy funding bucket. Although the funding, projects and award-paid ranger positions were maintained, Working on Country was no longer such a uniquely branded and managed land management program. However, its favourable reputation persists. A 2015 report (Pew Charitable Trusts and Synergies Economic Consulting, 2015) urged further expansion of the program, reconfirming that it is maintaining its ranger numbers and positive employment outcomes, with readily measurable social and economic paybacks to communities and governments alike.

In May 2016, the Australian Labor Party announced an election commitment to spend an extra $200 million over five years to double the number of Indigenous rangers under the Working on Country program. Once elected in July 2016, the Turnbull Liberal-Coalition Government continued the program at the existing level with no increase. In August 2016, the Minister for Indigenous Affairs, Nigel Scullion, confirmed a two-year extension of the project, to end June 2020.

By December 2017, however, the Government was still to renew contracts, creating a degree of uncertainty about future contracts for the 109 or so ranger projects supporting approximately 780 full time equivalent ranger jobs around Australia. This has created job uncertainty for the Indigenous rangers and the non-Indigenous program managers. The future of the program from 1 July 2020 appears intact, but this will require a commitment from the government of the day to ongoing funding.

**Illustration 5.2: Nolia Napangati Ward patch-burning on
Kiwirrkurra Indigenous Protected Area (WA), 2017**

Source: Dr Rachel Paltridge, for Kiwirrkurra IPA

5.3 Less successful policy: Home Insulation Program

The Home Insulation Program bids fair to become a classic study in public administration failure. Eighteen out of the 23 interviewees who rated this program considered it a failure, by far the highest number of failure nominations for any program that they chose to discuss. This section describes the program's origins, and the Royal Commission and other inquiries into its defects. Application of the Marsh and McConnell Framework also delivers a verdict of program failure.

Eighteen interviewees underlined the program's confusion of economic and 'green' objectives, unrealistic timeframes, weak consultation, poor oversight, poor staffing decisions and risk management, and poor handling of ministers and stakeholders. Discounting the political fallout, five other interviewees commended the successful stimulus effect and the insulation of over one million homes.

Added to the conflicting objectives, the Commonwealth had little mandate for the program, and flouted the stakeholder advice. While it could be said that the Environment Department received a 'hospital pass' from an imperious Executive and Prime Minister's Department, it too must incur some responsibility for the outcomes.

Home Insulation Program: Description

The Global Financial Crisis (GFC) hit Australia in September 2008. The Treasury head reportedly advised the Rudd Government to "Go hard, go early and go households" (Swan, April 9-10, 2011). After the first stimulus package, with its increase in the aged pension, the Government was keen to do more. A rebate to householders to encourage home insulation was seen as a high-benefit low-cost option. Home Insulation's origins as a relatively 'small' environment component (inside the $4.3 billion Energy Efficient Homes Package) of a huge ($42 billion) economic stimulus measure were to have grave consequences.

The program, by the time it was announced, had moved far away from the initial proposal. The Environment Department had proposed to Prime Minister and Cabinet a phased regional delivery by large and reputable firms over five years, with a co-contribution by households (Hindmoor and McConnell, 2013, 5; Australian Royal Commission into the Home Insulation Program 2014b, 222). This was rejected, in favour of an all-comers program to be delivered in two years flat.

The announced program variously aimed to: provide free ceiling insulation for 2.7 million homes; generate economic stimulus and support jobs for trades people and workers employed in residential ceiling insulation; improve the energy efficiency, comfort and value of homes; help households save an average of $200 per household per year on their heating and cooling energy bills; and reduce greenhouse gas emissions by around 40 million tonnes by 2020 (Department of Environment Water Heritage and the Arts, 2009; Prime Minister, 3 February 2009a, b).

Home Insulation Program: Results

The disintegration from a February 2009 stimulus measure to program termination in February 2010 was promptly examined by the Hawke Review (2010), a Senate Inquiry (Commonwealth of Australia, Senate, 2010) and an ANAO audit (2010). There were Coronial inquiries in NSW (Local Court of NSW, 4 October 2012) and Queensland (Office of the State Coroner, 4 July 2013) and other regulatory investigations. The Royal Commission Report (Australian Royal Commission into the Home Insulation Program, 2014a) gaped at the implied "fifteen-fold" increase in home insulation rates. It highlighted the tension between economic and environmental aims, the Environment Department being saddled with a cavalier delivery model. It pointed to poor risk management and compliance, permission of dangerous insulation, slack training requirements, and a casual reliance on State health and safety arrangements.

Table 5.2: Home Insulation Program, key events, 2007-2010

2007-2008

The Insulation Council of Australia and NZ was lobbying for home insulation subsidies.

A New Zealand Coroner criticised Government for not warning of home insulation dangers.

The Environment Department was analysing home insulation benefits.

COAG agreed to develop a National Strategy on Energy Efficiency.

February 2009

Prime Minister announced the Home Insulation Program, Phase 1, where householders had to get two quotes up front, and then got reimbursement of costs.

The Foil Insulation Association lobbied the PM to get foil included in the program.

The first industry consultation meeting heard that a similar NZ program had been suspended because of electrocutions. This meeting recommended mandatory installer training.

March-April 2009

Chief Executive of National Electrical Contractors wrote to Environment Minister re fire risks.

The Minter Ellison risk assessment was completed.

First program rebates were paid.

Table 5.2: Home Insulation Program, key events, 2007-2010 (cont.)

Queensland Building Services Authority warned Prime Minister's Department of safety risks.

The bureaucrats' 'Project Control Group' was established, to meet weekly.

Minter Ellison compiled the Risk Register, which omitted safety risks, and was not given to Minister.

June-July 2009

At the Industry Roundtable, the Department urged a low entry level for installers.

Payments began to be made *direct*, and online, to installer firms.

The Construction Industry Pocket Book on safe insulation was 'made available'.

Fire and injury-death risks were added to the Risk Register.

August-September 2009

First 'desktop' installer audits, and field inspections, took place.

The program budget was cut to $2.7 billion.

Installer firms first had to provide proof of insurance.

The Department first heard of a fire incident in the program.

October 2009

A review indicated there were emissions reporting errors in the program.

An electrocution occurred in Queensland, but the firm involved stayed in the program until 2010.

The Chief Executive of Master Electricians Australia wrote to and met with the Minister, urging the exclusion of foil insulation to prevent further deaths.

The Department reminded all installers of OH&S, linking the advice to the Pocket Book.

After meeting with industry, regulators, and training organisations, to discuss safety issues, the Department 'reviewed' the training package and revised the program guidelines.

Queensland banned the use of metal fasteners (in the program).

November-December 2009

The Minister announced a Queensland inspection of foil-insulated homes.

The program budget was re-cut, to $2.45 billion.

A 'Risk Committee' was hived off from the Project Control Group.

Another electrocution fatality occurred in Queensland.

The Department finally sent the 'Pocket Book' to all installers.

Another fatality – from heat exhaustion – occurred in NSW.

Further safety and consumer measures came in – plus a Deregistered Installer List.

The Minister announced mandatory training, for all installers.

An Approved Insulation Product List came into force.

February 2010

Queensland suffered a third electrocution fatality, the fourth fatality overall.

Minister finally bans foil insulation.

Calls for Minister's resignation are made in Senate Estimates.

The Government announced it would inspect all the foil-insulated homes.

The Government announced mandatory competencies, for all installers.

Claims paid numbered 1,114,000, at a cost of $1.47 billion.

The Hawke inquiry into the program was announced.

The program was terminated (19 February).

The program wind-up went into the Department of Climate Change and Energy Efficiency.

The ill-conceived implementation sprang from the Rudd Government's desire to inject stimulus funds quickly, to head off the Global Financial Crisis. The Minister (Arbib) coordinating the stimulus measures rejected any calls for caution. The program suffered from its conflicting and multiple objectives and a failure to heed expert advice. Key decisions were not based on evidence. The Environment Minister was not advised rigorously of changing circumstances. The incautious July 2009 shift to paying the installers directly triggered rapid program escalation, with rising fraud and safety breaches, and then the first installer death in October 2009.

This alarming unravelling (see Table 5.2) prompted an array of catch-up measures right up till February 2010, in terms of industry advice, industry insurance, more inspections, tougher risk assessment, mandatory training, and mandatory competencies. However, none of this reactive repair work seemed to be able to set right the shaky foundations, hence continuing bad publicity and the drastic step of program termination.

Assessment against the Marsh and McConnell Framework also implies program failure.

On the process dimension, there was a lack of documentation to support the policy proposal, with little consideration of safer and sounder policy options for the stimulus objective, a limited evidence base, a lack of consultation on the design and risks, plus limited (and unreliable) stakeholder input.

On the programmatic dimension, the results were mixed, as against stated objectives. The program was not efficiently targeted to achieve greater energy-efficiency or emissions-reduction aims at lesser costs, and less than half the target number of houses was insulated. Being 'good for the economy', it created thousands of temporary jobs at a time of great employment stress, which could be regarded as a 'positive' equity outcome, but there were four installer deaths and major collateral damage to the parent industry. There were significant installation defects, requiring a huge $700 million remediation.

It is on the political dimension that the failure is stark. The program was a front-page embarrassment for the Government over a protracted period. Despite the 2010 program termination for damage control, the Opposition continued to exploit the debacle, even two years after being re-elected in 2013.

The insulation industry and the Environment Department suffered major reputational damage. The political 'noise' had drowned out any messaging of the measurable economic and environment gains.

Home Insulation Program: Drivers of Failure

The big factors for policy success that are emphasised in the policy literature were strikingly absent in the design and implementation. A key factor less prominent in the literature – the agency of officials – also went missing in action.

Illustration 5.3: 'Home insulation program has closed'

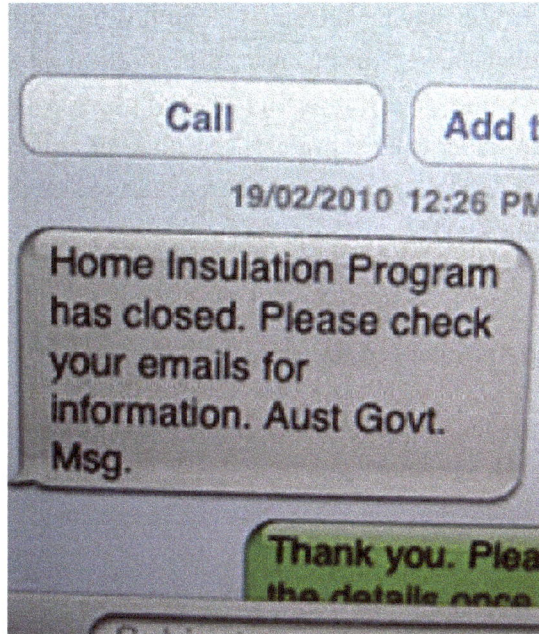

Source: *Brisbane Times*, photo, 19 Feb 2010

Contrary to the 'preconditions for success' in Chapter 2, there was no clear link between the nominal (energy) policy issue and the (home insulation) solution. The overriding stimulus objective required fast implementation, even if that meant poor quality installation and compromising the energy and environmental aims. The program was not targeted at the optimal *climatic* regions for the lowest unit cost of energy savings, and that meant environmental objectives were met at high financial cost.

Interviewees saw the main cause of failure in the origins of the program, with economic stimulus objectives distorting the program's shape and overrunning its 'green' objectives. "A policy process can fail," as one said, "if the politics overwhelm the clear evidence, as in the case of the Home Insulation Program."

Others recalled the early warning signs of failure, with little debate over the design, and risks being viewed through a Canberra lens rather than from a pragmatic business perspective:

> 'The Home Insulation Program was designed over a three-day period and announced so there was no scope to change... We had proposed a five-year rollout but the timeframe was reduced to two years and anyone could install, and it was crazy. Nothing was written down, so there was no scope to comment.'

> 'I asked, why are we, a general policy department, getting this large program to deliver in one of the most risky sectors? My family is in the housing business... I knew what the industry was like. We knew it was not controlled... The whole policy and program was just so poor. We had no selling points by then to counter... the media... After the first death, I recommended the program be closed down. I don't know how it was eventually closed down. Minister Garrett had reached that point, of wanting to close it down. He got no support from Rudd.'

Another interviewee confirmed that, once the design risks were flagged, the Department soldiered on, to implement the decision of the government of the day:

> 'The risk analysis did identify the problems... Government makes the decision. You get on with it. As problems arise you provide advice about some of the problems and potential solutions. You don't say, cut the program. In the end it was the right thing, to advise to terminate...'

Achieving the energy efficiency gains in a cost-effective way would have required a more controlled delivery. The Senate Inquiry (Commonwealth of Australia, Senate, 2010, 6.9) lamented the inherent ambiguity and conflicts in the program's objectives that contributed to a "monumental failure". Interviewees recalled how the economy and jobs quickly overrode the environmental objectives:

> 'Originally, it was an environment program but then it changed overnight to a stimulus program.'

> 'The [main] intent was job creation, not environment, and that was the fundamental flaw – everything stemmed from that.'

Stakeholder consultation, another strong recommendation in the policy literature, did occur, but ineffectually. Interviewees corroborated what the inquiries found, that consultation was procedural rather than genuine. The ANAO (2010, 26) found that the Prime Minister's Department forged ahead "with a sense of urgency", consulting little with the Environment Department or with industry. Safety concerns were written down in favour of industry enthusiasm, as the Queensland Coronial Inquiry found:

> "Unfortunately, electrical trades organisations... were not consulted earlier about the use of foil and metal staples in the program... The industry representatives who did participate in planning meetings seemed to

have been preoccupied with 'getting a slice of the pie' for their members..." (Office of the State Coroner, 4 July 2013, 68).

The Senate Inquiry (Commonwealth of Australia, Senate, 2010) noted there were warnings to Government about the electrical and fire risks as early as February 2009. Similarly, the Royal Commission report (Australian Royal Commission into the Home Insulation Program, 2014a, 3) complained that early warnings of insulation risks were ignored, even after the first death of October 2009.

Indeed, environment officials told the 2010 Senate Inquiry (Commonwealth of Australia, Senate, 2010, 3.10, 3.45, 3.57) that the risks of installing insulation in ceiling cavities were presented to the Government. Minister Garrett was warned by industry and peak body representatives and by State agencies (ANAO, 2010; Commonwealth of Australia, 2010, Section 3.57; Hawke, 2010; Office of the State Coroner, 4 July 2013). Those warnings were not heeded.

The decision to include foil insulation sidelined evidence then available in Australia and overseas. The peak body for foil installers wrote to the Prime Minister in February 2009 seeking inclusion of foil products (suited to tropical climates) and raising no concerns about the use of metal staples to fix insulation (Keeffe, 2014, 3). Including foil, when Queensland housing had a rate of faulty wiring around 30 per cent, and allowing inexperienced young installers, were recipes for high safety risks. The Government's hasty rollout, and its reluctance to favour or disfavour any part of the industry, kept the foil insulation in play (Keeffe, 2014, 3).

Inaction or indecisive interventions continued, even when the warnings began to come true. Royal Commission hearings (Australian Royal Commission into the Home Insulation Program 2014b, 252, 345, 1678-1730) implied that a key official neglected to brief Minister Garrett promptly and factually on the safety and fraud incidents mounting up between July and October 2009. At the Royal Commission May 12 2014 hearing, Garrett allowed that he became increasingly distrustful of his Department's advice.

The policy literature also urges a strong 'policy mandate', but the Commonwealth mandate here was dubious. Although the Commonwealth was providing the rebate, the evident risks to installers were blandly left with State agencies, with no extra support to manage the huge increase in installations. While the Commonwealth belatedly tried to re-regulate installers and to promote safety through its Industry Pocket Book (see Table 5.2), no federal portfolio had the inclination or the policy mandate to head off the obvious occupational safety implications of a sudden large surge in semi-skilled workers conducting dangerous work in confined spaces.

It was problematic that Home Insulation was an 'administered' program with no legislated mandate.

State Governments were usually the ones that legislated and supervised occupational health and safety, and industry and electrical regulation. Rebates for energy efficiency measures had usually been their province too. A Tier 1 interviewee said he initially pushed hard for States to deliver the program, as they "had the experience with these kinds of programs already and they were in charge of the regulatory framework in that space".

The Commonwealth adjudged itself as not responsible for safety risks, because the contracts lay between installers and households. Nominally, that put the responsibility for worker safety with the installer, and the responsibility for workplace safety and training with State regulatory agencies. The Queensland Coronial Inquiry didn't buy that line. As the Commonwealth had totally funded the program, it thereby shouldered a degree of responsibility that could not be transferred fully to third parties.

Rather more so than the formal inquiries, the interviews highlight the *absence* of officials exercising their proper agency as a factor limiting the scope for success.

At the outset, a braver Environment Department might have been able to negotiate, so as to sidestep carriage of the program altogether. Other departments did just that with risky stimulus measures proposed.

A couple of interviewees confessed that, when they realised what the delivery model entailed, they quietly moved jobs. Once the Department was lumbered with that model, its inadequate agency was also seen in the implementation.

Officials who were put into the key jobs were unsuitable. They failed to take advice on how to implement a program of that scale, failed to allocate early effort to compliance and audit, shirked sending bad news 'up the line', suffered from inadequate corporate systems, and diffused responsibility and accountability in large and unwieldy project committees.

Officials who held critical information, who were positioned to provide frank advice or to argue for policy variations, did not do so. In other words, there is an ethical aspect to the program's failure. Senior public servants will always face the moral and career temptations of telling ministers what (they imagine) ministers want to hear. Eventually, several officials faced uncomfortable moments in the Royal Commission, were cited adversely in its Report, or were cited confidentially.

At the time, both the officials and their political masters misread the extent to which relaxing of controls for faster implementation would be gamed by rogue operators:

'They were modelling and planning for what a reasonable person would do... You know, a reasonable person would have done it the way the public servants thought about it, but what if someone could see that a lot of money could be made and that opportunity may not come around again? Are they going to make the same decisions that I would with my very well paying job and the security that my job brings?'

This malfeasance, combined with householder frustration, shock-jock radio, and adversarial federal politics, proved a heady mix. Efforts to deliver environmental outcomes were overwhelmed by day-to-day crisis management of the political fallout.

Home Insulation Program: Postscript

As late as 2015, the Abbott Government advertised (Department of Industry and Science, 2015) compensation for firms adversely affected by the program. Yet the Rudd Government, some academic analyses, audits and inquiries, and five interviewees here, assessed aspects of the program as successful. It was perceived as moderating the impact of the GFC on Australia's economy. It did insulate around 1.1 million homes (less than one-third the initial projection) to the satisfaction of most households. The actual stimulus contribution, however, was never assessed. The program only accounted for about 6 per cent of the second stimulus package.

Whatever these positive aspects, the consensus of the formal inquiries, and the assessment derived from the Marsh and McConnell Framework, point to program failure. Surprisingly, this has received little scholarly attention.

A few academic analyses have cast the program as a clear failure and a prime example of poor public policy. Lewis (2010) commented that it failed the tests of good public policymaking. Tiffen (26 March 2010) wrote that the sources of failure lay deeper than the Federal Government, and that State agencies and installer businesses should shoulder some responsibility. Stewart and Mackie (2011) argued that the program failure could be understood in terms of the Government's optimistic belief that the risks had been 'outsourced' to State Governments and to installers.

As noted in Chapter 2, the IPAA (April 2012) assessed the program as failing to meet all ten of their tenets for good public policy. Kortt and Dollery (2012, 74) classified the program as a failure of government rather than policy. They said that a more measured implementation by State and local governments would have averted failure, though they acknowledged that the stimulus objectives wouldn't have been met. They also apportioned blame to the program managers, citing the Auditor-General's (ANAO, 2010, 82) assessment that officials had failed to manage and treat risk.

The scholarly view is that the program did not fail to quite the degree that the then Opposition claimed. Tiffen (26 March 2010) saw the media presentation of the program as unbalanced. He argued that the program had contributed to stimulus and energy efficiency objectives and that its sheer scale had exposed existing weaknesses in Australia's work safety regimes. On some matters at least, he said, the Government had acted promptly and properly. His judgment is backed up by the Queensland Coronial Inquiry, which found common elements in the three Queensland deaths. The employers had failed to discharge their safety responsibilities, and all three received convictions under electrical and workplace safety legislation (Office of the State Coroner, 4 July 2013, 64-66).

Less prominent in the external, academic autopsies is the key lesson from our insider interviews. That is, there is merit in officials staying resolute in their advice, even if it might cut against political and economic imperatives. If the officials had held the line, it is possible the Government might have looked for a less risky stimulus measure. Or, at least, the fallout of the one it chose could have been moderated. Home Insulation Royal Commissioner Hanger settled on a shortfall in the provision of "frank and fear-less" advice as a possible explanation of "what really went wrong and why".

Despite the huge program budget, the scope for the Environment Department officials to avoid failure and pursue a successful energy efficiency outcome was compromised by the drive for a rapid rollout from the Prime Minister's Department, reinforced by pressure from Minister Arbib and the Office of the Coordinator General. Experienced program managers, fearing likely failure, stepped away from involvement.

Could this once-in-a-generation level of program failure happen again? The answer to that perhaps lies as much in the constants of human nature as it does in the widely accepted conventions for successful policy development. The ancient term *hubris* is one way to describe the predisposition that appeared to lead Government Ministers and their central officials away from the grounding policy precepts. To be sure, some key figures paid the price of public censure, but one or two were also promoted.

Interestingly, VET FEE-HELP, for vocational education and training, began to be compared with Home Insulation (Bachelard et. al, 16 September 2015). It too was (a) an uncapped program making (b) poorly audited direct payments to (c) poorly regulated private providers who were (d) targeting their clients carelessly. It was duly scrapped the following year (Australian Financial Review, 7 October 2016).

5.4 Less successful policy: Sustainable Population Strategy

Though not among the original 12 target policies and programs, the Sustainable Population Strategy of 2010-2011 was chosen as the fourth case study. Like the Home Insulation Program, it is particularly instructive, in that it divided the officials, and illustrated the potential pitfalls of top-down policy, where measured or evidence-based policy formulation struggles to make a dent on the political imperatives.

Contrary to the 'preconditions for success' in Chapter 2, there was but a tenuous link between the nominal policy issue (population) and the eventual solutions (suburban, regional, and road programs). Rather, the 'solutions' fit in with the language used at the outset by Ministers to frame the issues, such language discounting wider community views that had been a key trigger for the policy process.

Assessment of the Strategy against the Marsh and McConnell Framework locates it as mixed outcomes at best, or towards failure. Whatever political success it had is offset by its poor policy and program results.

Sustainable Population Strategy: Description

The published Strategy (Commonwealth of Australia, 2011) could almost be said to derive from a single incident. Prime Minister Rudd was televised in 2009 responding to the heady population projections in the imminent third Intergenerational Report (Commonwealth of Australia, 2010). "I actually believe in a big Australia," he commented, "I make no apology for that." (O'Connor and Lines, 2010, 2).

It's no secret that Australia's population has grown strongly and reliably since World War II, with the surge from about 2005 onwards primarily due to a migration spike. In the 40 years to 2010, growth averaged 1.4 per cent per annum (Commonwealth of Australia, 2011, 14). That rose to 1.7 per cent during the 2005-2013 period (Krockenberger, 2015, 14). Krockenberger also shows that, among all OECD nations, only Luxembourg and Israel exceeded Australia's figure of 1.7 per cent. The other four major English-speaking nations, United States, United Kingdom, Canada, and New Zealand, also traditional advocates of high population growth, were clustered around 1 per cent or less.

At the time, Rudd was only reflecting settled bipartisan policy. Yet his remarks were controversial and affected his popularity. As one senior interviewee noted:

> 'It was a perfect storm. Rudd didn't go through Cabinet with the [population] policy. At the same time people were concerned about traffic congestion in western Sydney, in outer Melbourne, in Perth, in Brisbane. There were concerns about migration pressures on the urban fringes.'

It appears that Rudd's error was to articulate the policy all too clearly, as compared with the norm of "virtual silence" or "little public debate" (Krockenberger, 2015, 3). The story of the Strategy is largely that of steering the ship back to the quiet zone.

Responding to the public reaction, Rudd appointed Tony Burke as Australia's first 'Population Minister' in April 2010 (ABC News, 3 April 2010). Quickly Rudd signalled his preferred approach, "Mr Rudd says…the impact of population changes on regional Australia will be an early priority". Rudd's successor, Julia Gillard, advocated a 'Sustainable Australia' and not 'Big Australia' (ABC News, 16 May 2011). The finished form of the 2011 Strategy (Commonwealth of Australia, 2011) suggests she was revising the terminology rather more than the policy itself.

In July 2010, Burke "established three advisory panels to advise him on sustainable population issues… from three different viewpoints: demography and liveability; productivity and prosperity; and sustainable development" (Department of the Environment, 2015c). He then released an Issues Paper (Department of Sustainability Environment Water Population and Communities, 2010) for public comment. To set the tone, his accompanying press release (Department of the Environment, 2015b) makes *seven* references to "population *change*" [author emphases]. "Policy for a sustainable Australia," he declared, "begins with the principle of regional difference".

In its 15 consultation questions, the Issues Paper defers to the Minister's line, avoiding substantive discussion of national population data, choices, or policy arrangements. "Since the 1970s," it asserts, "all population inquiries sponsored by Australian Governments have rejected the notion of a population target or national carrying capacity." As it happens, sobering information about the condition of the driest continent could have been drawn from his own Department's five-yearly *State of the Environment* series (see State of the Environment Committee 2011, 2011).

The same claim about population inquiries is repeated in the 2011 Strategy. This also asserts (Commonwealth of Australia, 2011, 24) that governments "cannot accurately predict or directly control" population. Krockenberger's (2015) analysis undermines that claim.

That is to say, Australia has long had policies (in effect, located in the Treasury and Immigration Departments) delivering fairly predictable population growth around 1.4-1.5 per cent per annum. Whenever the graph shifts much away from that mark, this is less because of 'unpredictable' trends in domestic increase, and more because of government's deliberately 'demand driven' changes in migration levels.

Like the Issues Paper, the Strategy avoids serious data or discussion on Australian population trends and population policy. It elides the very change that was already well under way at the time, that is, roughly a doubling of net overseas migration. It avoids international comparisons, especially in relation to prosperous countries with lower population growth, whether by attrition or by design. Placing the answer ahead of the question, it takes as a given the unalloyed economic (skills) and social (demographic) benefits of Australia's past and present "robust" migration program. It presumably does likewise with domestic policies and payments that might influence Australian family formation and size, although these are neither mentioned nor reviewed.

In effect, the Strategy follows the 'Treasury line'. This is hardly surprising, as a Treasury Band 2 (a Tier 2 as this book calls it) and supporting staff were seconded in to the Environment Department to direct its Population Taskforce (see attendees, Parliament of Australia, 18 October 2010). The published Strategy returns to the Minister's theme that population policy is regional policy by another name. Its specific new measures were only worth $230 million over four years (Urbanalyst, 2011). The main components were the Suburban Jobs Program ($100 million), Managed Motorways ($61 million), Sustainable Regional Development ($29 million), Liveable Cities ($20 million), Measuring Sustainability ($10 million) and Promoting Regional Living ($12 million). The Strategy also recapitulated $4.3 billion in existing 2011-12 Budget "investment in regions", and referred to other measures to boost "regional migration", particularly extra places for Regional Sponsored Migration.

Again, this regional policy was optimistic, and quite at adds with the underlying evidence. Ever since World War II, Australia has been very successful at population growth, but very unsuccessful at channelling that growth into non-capital city regions. Nearly nine out of ten Australians now live in urban areas, one of the highest proportions of any country, and 75 per cent are in cities of 100,000 or more (Commonwealth of Australia, 2011, 32). Over 2003-2013, the Australian population (migration) boom was overwhelmingly directed towards the four big cities of Sydney, Melbourne, Brisbane and Perth (Krockenberger, 2015, 11).

Sustainable Population Strategy: Results

The Environment Department (2015d) 'Sustainable population' homepage has documented modest outcomes. The Suburban Jobs Program, although pared to $45 million by 2014, was said to be building three projects on big-city fringes. Some research and reporting for Measuring Sustainability has taken place. Limited funding appears to have been rolled out, for Managed Motorways and Liveable Cities.

As for the other investment and migration measures adduced in the Strategy, there is little evaluation or evidence to suggest that these could have had any major impact on the economic and cultural factors that continue to place migrants (and native born Australians) largely in capital and other cities. Regional Sponsored Migration certainly did increase (Department of Immigration and Border Protection, 2015), from 11,100 places in 2010-11 to 16,500 in 2013-2014, but here the definition of 'regional' allows most major cities apart from Sydney, Melbourne and Brisbane.

By 2013, the term 'population' had been erased once again from the Environment Department's title and from the named functions in its organisation chart.

That didn't mean that Australia had deleted population policy itself. It just meant that the policy had reverted to the norm of little overt discussion. The main population policy levers remained within the Treasury. The main population program levers remained with the migration intakes of the Department of Immigration and Border Protection. Neither receives much in the way of parliamentary or public scrutiny.

Assessment of the Strategy against the Marsh and McConnell Framework implies mixed results at best, or verging towards failure.

On the surface, the process dimension is impressive, with three advisory panels, a call for submissions, and an issues paper. On closer scrutiny, this process is more pro forma than genuine. Echoing Home Insulation, this was partly due to the interventions of the Prime Minister's Department.

The advisory panels looked diverse, but they excluded any prominent figures and authorities known to disagree with then-current policies. One senior interviewee warmly commended the panel process, but regretted that their work was "buried" when the Prime Minister's Department decreed at short notice a bland Issues Paper with a "lot of pictures and not many words".

Whatever the input from the panels and the (380) submissions, the diversionary tactics of "population *changes*" and "*regional* Australia" articulated in Rudd's first press release dominated the process and the final Strategy. This Strategy too was "worked on" by the Prime Minister's Department, as confirmed by an interviewee.

On the programmatic dimension, the results were poor. In effect, Big Australia was taken as read as an unalloyed 'good for the economy'. There was no airing of its pros and cons (as found in O'Connor et al., 2012) or of any potential alternatives. Questions about the real beneficiaries of high population growth, or indeed the environmental implications, were set aside. Starved of genuine policy intent, the Strategy reverted to a patchwork of regional programs. As one interviewee put it:

> 'The question was really, how do we get it off the agenda? So some funds were given to Burke for work, as a thank you for doing that.'

The political dimension was a success, although one largely defined by getting the issue off the agenda. Ironically, although the Minister launched his growth-friendly Strategy at a Gold Coast Housing Industry Association event (Architecture and Design, 2011), still he attracted criticism from the Opposition, the Property Council of Australia, and the Australian Industry Group.

Sustainable Population Strategy: Drivers of Failure

Factors for policy success emphasised in the policy literature played only a weak hand. The policy origins, objectives, and evidence, were narrow. Consultation was broader, but what it produced found little place in the final policy outcomes. The Environment officials who were nominally responsible for the policy development took a backseat to the seconded Treasury team.

The top-down origins of the policy constrained success. It sprang largely from the Prime Minister's remark and the resulting pressures he faced. His Department and the Treasury set the pace, rather than the nominally responsible Environment Department.

Even though voter reactions to 'Big Australia' had been a policy trigger, the process avoided unpacking the reasons for this reaction. It commissioned no opinion surveys of its own. As an out, the final Strategy blandly noted "a divergence of views as to whether population and immigration should be increased or stabilised." But surveys available from 2010 to 2017 generally suggest considerable levels of voter resistance to the prescribed policies of high immigration and high population growth.

For example, the 2010 ANU Australian Survey of Social Attitudes (ABC News, 14 April 2010) had 69 per cent thinking Australia didn't need more people. Betts' (2015) voter sample found that 51 per cent thought Australia did not need more people. Of the 31 per cent who thought it did, nearly half wanted to keep the population under 30 million.

The 2014 Lowy Institute survey (Monash University, 2015) found much the same as the corresponding survey of 2010. Sixty-four per cent of respondents favoured a target population of 30 million or less, well below any figure available in any Treasury 'projections' for the mid 21st century. Australia Institute (Krockenberger, 2015, 4) polling of 2014 said, "around half of all Australians think population is growing too fast and we should have a national debate". Essential Reports of 2013 (Monash University, 2015) had 45 per cent of those sampled thinking population growth was too fast, 42 per cent thought it was about right or too slow.

The 2016 Scanlon surveys (Markus, 2016) claim increasing support for migration over the past 10-15 years, just 34 per cent now finding it "too high".

A 2016 Essential Report (Essential Media, 4 October 2016) of similar sample size does not agree. There, 50 per cent still thought immigration over the previous ten years was "too high" with 28 per cent on "about right" and 12 per cent on "too low".

Continuing the 'duelling surveys', Betts and Birrell (2017) find 54 per cent wanting a reduction in migration while 2017 Scanlon (Markus, 2017) has just 40 per cent (up from 34 per cent in 2016) finding migration too high, that is, they want a reduction. Betts and Birrell posit that, setting aside that theirs is a voter survey versus the Scanlon resident survey, it may be that attitudes have hardened, even since 2016.

Linked to its political origins, the policy process of 2010-11 held to narrow objectives and narrow evidence. From the outset, the mantras were "population change" and "regional Australia". Despite a professional advisory and consultation process, the politics sanitised the results, taking them out of the Issues Paper and final Strategy.

In this politicised process, the 'agency' of Environment officials had limited impact. Larger forces were controlling the play. In their first uses of terminology, the Prime Minister and the Environment Minister clearly telegraphed what it was they wanted to see at the end of the process. To that effect, the Prime Minister's Department and the Treasury, rather than the Environment Department, shaped the policy writing.

Instructively, two senior interviewees (both Tier 2-and-up) construed the Strategy quite differently. The first regarded Australia's population level as a fundamental issue, if environment policy was ever going to make any real difference. He saw the politicised crafting of the Strategy as a rare opportunity that unfortunately had gone begging:

> 'You know the bad policy. Population policy was one of them. It should be quickly buried in a dark, dark corner of Australia's public policy history. It was a bitter pill for me to have to swallow as compared to being able to do it properly. There was never any attempt to do it properly. Therefore you know it wouldn't be successful. But what is the measure of success? Some stakeholders celebrated the outcome. It was a success for the Government.'

By contrast, the second argued that the Department's best course of action lay in its tempering an exercise that had begun with a call to significantly increase Australia's population for economic growth. The Strategy had taken the heat out of the issue and, so he claimed, may well have avoided even higher population growth:

> 'Sometimes policy is successful in that it avoids 4th or 5th best outcome, and it helped to defuse the public debate around population, although that could arise at any point in time. As a policy document and a set of initiatives it is lacklustre and was criticised as such, it could have had more rigour in terms of the data. I don't consider it a crowning achievement but I consider it has been successful in the context.'

It's debatable that the Department actually headed off a more expansive outcome. Driven by higher migration, Australian population grew faster in 2012, 2013, and 2014, than it had in 2011 (Krockenberger, 2015, 7). The contentious population forecasts of the 2010 Intergenerational Report were ramped up even more in its 2015 successor (Commonwealth of Australia, 2015b). Such figures imply that the Strategy's success was more in political terms, less in policy or programmatic terms.

Sustainable Population Strategy: Postscript

To paraphrase the late John Lennon, perhaps Australian population policy is what just 'happens', while you are busy making other plans.

Prime Minister Rudd had got into some difficulty by, in effect, drawing attention to the routinely high migration and population assumptions in the Intergenerational Report of 2010. But, by 2015, the 2015 Federal Budget (Commonwealth of Australia, 2015a, 97-98) and the 2015 Intergenerational Report (Commonwealth of Australia, 2015b) were applying *even higher* assumptions.

The 2015 Budget assumes net overseas migration of *250,000* in each of 2016 to 2018. It and the Report apply the usual pretext that Australian population is 'projected' rather than planned. The Report has population rising from 24 million to 40 million by 2055. But such an increase would largely be driven by conscious government policy – an assumed net overseas migration of 215,000 *every year* up to 2055.

Retreating slightly, the 2016 (Commonwealth of Australia, 2016, 95-96) and 2017 (Commonwealth of Australia, 2017, 87-88) Budgets assume annual net migration of 203,000-225,000 over 2016-2019, annual population growth around 1.5-2 per cent.

These projected migration figures are comparable to the annual migration levels that have applied since 2007, but roughly *twice as high* as the levels of 2000 up to 2006.

In effect, this amounts to a substantial policy change. While such a change has bipartisan support, it has never been taken to the electorate. At 2017, neither the Liberal nor Labor website revealed any explicit or substantive national policies on population or immigration. Rather, both sides tacitly agree to take the high population growth 'projections' of the federal budget as a given in the economic policy furniture. In New Zealand, by contrast, Labour broke ranks with the Nationals and put in its election platform (New Zealand Labour, 2016) a 30-40% migration cut.

As it happened, the 2015 Intergenerational Report referred to by Rudd was poorly received, though not necessarily for its population settings. While primarily critiquing the implausible tax assumptions,

Denniss (5 March 2015) queried the infrastructure cost implications of such large population increases. Betts (13 March 2015), who had been one of Minister Burke's advisory panellists, challenged the assumed link between population and prosperity. Continually ratcheting up GDP numbers, she argued, did little for GDP per capita or for personal wellbeing. Recent data from 32 OECD nations showed "no statistically significant association between productivity and population growth".

Rather disguising the actual policy settings, the Abbott Government merged the Immigration and Customs agencies into 'Immigration and Border Protection'. Thus, a single Department was pursuing a vigorous migration policy at the same time as a punitive asylum policy (Hartcher, 1 September 2015). Further obscuring these settings (Tingle, 21 July 2017), it was announced mid 2017 that DIBP itself would be wrapped up into a new 'Home Affairs' super-agency.

This section has aimed to discuss population policy 'success' and 'failure' rather than the population policies themselves being 'right' or 'wrong'. But first it has had to reassert the simple point that Australia *does indeed* have defined, longstanding population policies, however much these may be denied. Indeed, claims still appear (Allen, 3 July 2017) that Australia "doesn't have" an overarching population policy.

In such terms, the 2011 Strategy defaulted a rare opportunity to (at least) air our population policies or to (frankly) review them. This default was lent fresh relevance by Sydney and Melbourne, easily the main migrant destinations in our near OECD-leading population growth rates, moving into the world's 10 least affordable major housing markets (Bourke, 24 February 2017).

As a final note, coyness about population policy is a global and not just an Australian phenomenon. The revised United Nations Sustainable Development Goals (UNDP, 2015) cover environmental sustainability in terms of climate change, terrestrial ecosystems and oceans. Remarkably, they avoid mentioning human population *altogether*, as a (or the) key influence over environmental sustainability, even though the UN itself and other newer projections have that population exceeding 11 billion globally by 2100 (Carrington, 26 September 2014).

Chapter 6

Future Avenues to Environment Policy Success

At the beginning, this project centred on whether or not federal environment policy officials had a sense of what policies would succeed and what factors would drive success. Referring to the case studies, this final chapter extends three themes that have emerged during the project research.

The first theme is that the project tested and validated new measures in the underexplored field of 'policy success'. Secondly, it highlighted the concerted 'agency' of officials as an unexpectedly important factor in such success.

Finally, it illustrated useful tactics to win success in Australian environment policy. Adept officials associated 'green' policies with bigger agendas, invented lateral ploys to free up policies, and practised the policymaker's habits of patience and perseverance.

6.1 Better measures of policy success

Chapter 2 surveyed the thinking behind the main concepts of policy success and failure. It found in the literature over the years an intense interest in the preconditions for policy success, and the advance factors that might indicate or drive policy success.

Table 2.1 summarised the changing trends in policy theory since the 1950s. This begins with the 'rationality' of 1950s policy science and its idealised policy 'cycle', and moves to 1970s ideas of agenda

Succeeding and Failing in Australian Environment Policy

setting and 'evidence based' policymaking. It concludes with more recent whole-of-government ideas, where policy is construed as a 'wicked' or risky problem that might need to be tackled broadly through partnerships, networks and collaboration.

Not finding any one broad theory to be a satisfactory guide, this project also examined the extensive literature on specific factors that drive policy success. This generated a useful list of success factors at Table 2.2. These were applied in Chapter 4, as a reference point for the interviewees' opinions about predictors of success and failure.

Much less a feature of the literature is the other side of the policy-theory coin, not that of predicting policy success, but that of assessing continuing or completed policies for their levels of success (or failure).

It has to be acknowledged that program 'success' or 'failure' is an elusive and multi-layered concept, and that success may look different at different points along the program life cycle. For example, even the star-crossed Home Insulation Program may look better over a longer arc of time, as its modest program (insulation) benefits persist.

Nevertheless, we argue that program success and failure is an important practical topic that receives too little outside scrutiny. While Home Insulation was terminated abruptly, this was unusual, and partly due to the sheer newsworthiness of its fraud incidents and its industrial accidents. It is also depressingly common for large programs of doubtful efficiency or equity to persist seemingly immune to review over long periods.

Of course, government itself has its traditions of during- or after-the-fact policy or program evaluation and audit, also discussed in Chapter 2.

The 'performance' audit is usually performed by an agency external to the program department. Yet other issues may cloud its robustness. The more searching an audit is, the less it may attract the program agency's buy-in. To be sure, there can still be tough audits of failed programs. The ANAO audit of Home Insulation has been cited as one of these.

The performance auditor may also be hampered if the original outcome measures set up by the program department are bland or process-oriented, failing to cut through to the critical aspects of success or failure. For example, if a program is essentially a buy-off or a settlement for a particular or influential interest group, there may not be too strenuous an effort to set up inquisitive or demanding outcome measures that might adequately reflect broader community interests and priorities.

External or academic interest in policy success is, as noted, rather recent. After some searching, this project settled on the recently developed Marsh and McConnell Framework as a useful tool. By assessing policy success along process, programmatic and political dimensions, this tool has begun to gain some currency with researchers. Van Assche et al. (2011) applied it in challenging government claims of 'success' in Netherlands land use planning. The UK Institute of Government (Rutter et al., 2012) applied it to a major examination of six successful UK policies. Newman (2014) used Marsh and McConnell to review policy success in transport systems.

This research therefore adopted the Marsh and McConnell Framework, as an orderly and useful external means for re-assessing the validity of program successes and failures as nominated 'subjectively' by the interview group.

Hence, the main report of the research (Chapter 3) culminates in Table 3.2. This rechecks and revalidates the interviewee assessments of the 12 target programs from a Marsh and McConnell perspective. In so doing, it tweaks previous applications of Marsh and McConnell, recognising and enumerating the real world 'mixed outcomes' that lie in between the more evident successes and the more evident failures.

That being said, the interviewees' assessments of success/mixed outcomes/failure are generally re-confirmed. The partial exception is Home Insulation, where a small minority of interviewees swam against the majority verdict of program failure. There is an extended consideration of the history of this case in Chapter 5. Partly by application of Marsh and McConnell, this comes down strongly in favour of the majority.

We take these results as a fresh indication of the usefulness of trying to measure program success and failure. Also confirmed is the usefulness of the Marsh and McConnell Framework for such efforts, especially when 'mixed outcomes' are added in to the black and white of 'failure' and 'success'.

Encouragingly, researchers applying the Framework have also suggested tinkering with it. For example, Crowley and Walker (2012, 8) suggested a fourth dimension of 'policy context' for environment policy applications of the Framework. Including the context, they argued, would allow ecological considerations to be factored in to assessments of success and failure. Based on this research, we lean towards a slightly different extension of the Framework.

As developed (Table 2.3), the Framework does include the idea of the 'actor/interest' (in effect, which groups win or lose) as an 'indicator' to be examined under the programmatic dimension. This 'fairness' or 'equity' dimension, we suggest, is worthy of elevation as a dimension of policy and program success in its own right.

For one thing, now evident in Australia and other OECD nations is a general retreat from the fairer distributions of wealth and income that applied from the early part of the 20th century up until the 1970s. Piketty (2014) has popularised this influential analysis, which says the rate of return to (private) capital will tend to beat the rate of economic growth over the long run. Reich (2015) offers another major reflection, on the negative implications of market power for social equality. A bolder formulation of these types of ideas is Di Muzio's political economy of the "growing gap between the [top] 1% and the rest of humanity" (Di Muzio, 2015). By implication then, policy and program design is not so well advised, to assume that a rising economic tide will lift all boats, and thereby play down or overlook equity concerns and equity chasms.

In Australia, the big adverse reaction to the 2014 Federal budget is a recent, graphic illustration of the risks of rolling over the top of the equity or 'winners and losers' dimensions of policy. Like it or not, the community clearly perceived intended health and higher education 'reforms' as onerous and unfair, and reacted vigorously.

Our case studies illustrate analogous effects. Home Insulation and the Sustainable Population Strategy both suffered from an over-generalised assumption that the simple expansiveness of 'good for economic growth' would also be a robust or sufficient indicator of a specific environment program's merit or success.

Conversely, Working on Country consciously targeted disadvantaged minority groups, and deliberately broke with budget orthodoxy, so as to resource these groups adequately. Sitting somewhere in the middle of these two extremes is Fuel Quality Standards. It achieved the unusual 'win-win' of both economic and environment gains, and major gains or losses in equity did not appear to be crucial considerations.

Whether by extensions of Marsh and McConnell, or by the use of other tools, we urge external researchers and commentators to hold governments to better account for their policy and program successes and failures. Government audit and evaluation, in our view, lacks adequate coverage of programs and is constrained by political and agency sensitivities from doing the task thoroughly. Some officials themselves, in our Home Insulation and Sustainable Population examples, were seen to judge programs as 'successful', merely or primarily because they blandly served the government agenda or the market agenda.

Sustained external scrutiny may have a particular role, whenever a tacit bipartisan consensus tends to close down the political discussion of policy alternatives that are not favoured by vested interests. The Sustainable Population Strategy case study is a clear example of this. A similar example in education policy is the funding for non-government schools, readily accepted by both major parties as a top-ten program (over $11 billion in 2017-18) in the Federal budget.

Examples are also readily available in economic and tax policy, where a common view (see Bongiorno, 2015) is that national 'economic reform' has stalled somewhat since the dollar float and other notable deregulatory measures of the 1980s.

6.2 Officials as agents for policy success

In this study, the term 'agency' means the self-directed actions of officials to use policy to achieve a particular result for the good of the environment.

The central finding was that the sustained exercise (or not) of this kind of agency was a most important, if not the most important, predictor of success (or not) of policies.

When officials applied themselves creatively and tenaciously, as they did in Working on Country, success was that much more likely, despite the prior history of failure in Indigenous policy. When they did not, as in Home Insulation, the risks of failure were greater, even when there were lavish resources available.

As discussed, this does not mean that officials simply looked in the mirror and saw themselves as the key to successful outcomes. On the contrary, they played down the success of programs that they themselves had been involved in.

Tellingly, they added that their fellow officials who could cut through to get these successful policy outcomes were not the routine or the norm. They were more like the surprising minority. Relatively few "inside runners", they commented, had the nous to ask the right policy questions. Intrinsic policy flair was not readily teachable, because "some people never get policy". Also, it did not necessarily follow that the individuals most effective at getting policy results would be the high-ranking SES officers.

The interview subjects did not see policy entrepreneurship to be at odds with public service values and ethics. They saw the *judicious* exercise of agency as a legitimate and healthy aspect of new-policy formulation. Much of policy was essentially seen to be "devised and crafted" inside the public service.

The idea of policy agency can be reconsidered against a major reform blueprint for the Australian Public Service, *Ahead of the Game* (Advisory Group on Reform of Australian Government Administration, 2010). This said that a high-performing public service should have "strong leadership and strategic direction" with a "highly capable workforce". It criticised the stingy APS spend on talent development, relative to best practice in private sector firms.

Since then, most of the key APS departments have taken part in a major program of capability reviews (Australian Public Service Commission, 2015). Once again, a number of these reviews urge the improvement of policy development skills inside the department.

The findings here are not inconsistent with the directions of these reviews, but there are provisos. As identified in our research, policy agency is not so much a tribal APS skill, but rather more an elusive skill that may be nurtured from time to time in certain departments among certain individuals or small groups.

The senior journalist Laura Tingle (2015) has given a timely, if pessimistic, assessment of the retained APS capacity to offer excellent policy advice. She sees that capacity as being diminished over the past 30 years by factors such as the decline of cabinet government, the rise of ministerial advisers, periodic axing of very senior public servants, and loss of institutional memory caused by more frequent agency-hopping for promotion. Former public service chief Terry Moran (2013) expressed similar concerns about the politicisation or marginalisation of the public services.

Our findings about the benefits of 'agency' go less to these general concerns about institutional or cultural decline in the public service. They go more to the moral and ethical dimensions of public service – as may be inferred by what senior officials do or do not do, when faced with genuinely tough or potentially career-limiting choices.

It may be that the late 1940s up until the 1980s was a golden era in the independence and robustness of public service advice. Nevertheless, this study implies that the externally driven decline of the public service can be overstated, as the public service retains large capacities to exercise (or fail to exercise) resolute agency to encourage successful and equitable policy outcomes. While governments retain leeway to 'reward or punish' senior officials for their perceived policy successes or otherwise, so too does the public service itself.

Returning to Home Insulation, the analysis uncovered *three* separate phases of absence of agency. Firstly, the Environment Department tacitly accepted a fraught economic-stimulus program, when other departments managed to avoid similar programs. Secondly, senior officials quietly decamped, as they reasonably suspected the stimulus-at-all-costs model imposed on the Department was dangerous or unworkable. Thirdly, once the program had begun, unsuitable officials were placed in key positions. Some of these baulked from giving honest and timely advice.

6.3 Succeeding in environment policy

Chapter 1 identified a generally pessimistic long-term view in the Australian environment policy literature whereby Australia's ingrained 'development at all costs' economic imperatives routinely overrule the application of prudent long-term environmental policy. Government's own five-yearly State of the Environment reports have struggled to paint optimistic pictures of the long-term trends. The 2011 report cited clear and current extinction dangers among the Northern Australia mammals, but these got short shrift in the Northern Australia White Paper of 2015.

Nevertheless, Chapter 1 also came back to the view that the new kind of federal involvement in environment policy since the 1970s *had* led to slower declines in environment quality *or* had delivered measurable improvements in environment quality. Examples of the first kind were more common in 'green' environment policies such as protection of iconic areas, expansion of parks and reserves, and rollbacks on clearing of native vegetation and forests. Examples of the second kind were more common in what interviewees referred to as 'brown' environment policies such as ozone protection, urban air quality, water quality and fuel quality.

To the extent that this study offers lessons for pursuing better environment policy outcomes, what might these be? One lesson is already implied by the point above – that 'brown' environment policies will tend to do better than 'green'. Commonly, this is because the officials crafting 'brown' policies are able to deliver directly the win-win of better environment outcomes that do not impede or may be seen to boost all-important 'economic growth' – Fuel Quality again. That is not so easy to achieve with a 'green' policy that ostensibly does little for economic growth or may be seen to impede it. That explains why the officials crafting Working for Country hitched a tactical ride on a larger socio-economic bandwagon, while having some confidence that they could build up the biodiversity and Indigenous-health evidence over time.

Pragmatically, this suggests that environment policy will be boosted when it can find respectable links to larger agendas of greater political appeal, be they in climate change, or in other mainstream areas of socio-economic policy. Both Fuel Quality and Working on Country suggest that such links can be made in ways that do not unduly corrupt or 'marketise' the underlying environment goals.

On the other hand, the linking may be problematic for the underlying environment goals. One example is the dubious environmental 'covenants' or 'offsets' (see ABC Radio National, 16 March 2014) that are meant to compensate for land disturbance and vegetation clearing in mining or other developments. Another example is the convenient but contestable (see Bennet, 2015; Böhm, 12 April 2013) assumption that market-based schemes are the best bet to reduce greenhouse gas emissions.

A second lesson is that environment policy may benefit from employing the actual tactics with which interviewees illustrated the idea of 'agency'. These tactics include the lateral-thinking ploys that officials invented to clear the pathway in particular cases. Examples were land-clearing moratoriums into Commonwealth-State agreements, invoking the *EPBC Act* to unlock marine protection policy, and paying Indigenous people award wages in caring for country.

Such tactics may not be easy to teach, as they depend to some extent on the flair and creativity of individual officers who happen to be in key positions at critical turning points.

Other tactics that are wrapped up in the idea of agency are perhaps more teachable and learnable, in that they are more like general habits of perseverance than particular flashes of insight. In Chapter 4, these included extreme patience in sowing policy seeds, deep knowledge of external stakeholder positions to overcome opposition to new policies, massaging the policy objectives, and resolution in the face of inconclusive evidence.

6.4 Conclusion

This crux of this book has been whether or not federal environment policy officials have a sense of what policies will succeed or fail and what factors drive success.

The concept of 'success' (rather than failure) was in itself successful.

It more than anything else generated deep reflections on the part of the 51 Environment Department interviewees, about which environment policies, if any, actually worked and why so. Their insights imply that public policy theory would do well to be more inclusive of the intentions and strategies of officials, in steering policy away from failure and towards success. Such roles tend to fall outside the radar of externally located studies and evaluations of Australian environmental policy, which not unreasonably find little evidence of lasting success.

Notably, nearly all the interviewees struggled to define exactly what it is that 'policy' means. But they all agreed that success in environment policy required making a tangible environmental difference, or at least minimising the environmental harm. Ninety per cent agreed it was possible to predict whether or not a particular policy would succeed. They were more inclined to predict success if there was a strong policy mandate and negatively affected interests had been placated or compensated.

The interview transcripts, and the canny ploys they revealed in the case studies of particular policy episodes, confirmed the importance of nuanced stakeholder consultations, the setting of clear objectives, and a sound evidence base. Of the well-known success factors in the literature, these presented as perhaps the most important ones for practitioners in the environment policy context.

Over and above these well-known factors, the 'agency' of officials was an unexpected and at times subterranean factor driving success. While the evidence of such behaviour usually had to be inferred from the transcripts, several interviewees commented directly that individuals with real policy flair are uncommon.

The study found that interviewees generally agreed on which programs were successful, mixed in outcomes, or failed, and their assessments generally aligned with those derived externally by applying the Marsh and McConnell Framework.

These findings reinforce Wildavsky's much earlier and seminal findings in the *Art and Craft of Policy Analysis* (1979). He understood why not everyone could do policy, as it requires creativity and a tolerance for ambiguity. He observed that assessing policy success or failure involves judgment rather than scientific precision.

As a caution, the findings here derive from a particular policy era. The two decades that were being researched started in the mid-1990s, when the federal Environment Minister first began to be a regular member of Cabinet, and his Department first began to flex its authority to fashion nationally significant policies and programs.

With the present and future pace of policy, there may be less scope for the policy 'waiting game' of patience and perseverance played out here by the abler officials. Nevertheless, the applicability of the findings could be tested in other federal policy contexts.

The so-called 'central agencies', which dominate budget and economic policy, and overall policy formulation, are one obvious context. Health and education also appeal, as they too have complex and mixed Commonwealth and State roles, and they may also attract committed officials more able to exercise 'agency' when it is required.

Appendix: Interview questions

Interviewer: **Kathleen Mackie. PhD student. UNSW.**

Topic: **Federal environment policymaking: Indicators of success.**

Interview questions for use with senior environment policymakers.

Lead in statement:

'I am interested in the process of policymaking with a specific focus on federal environment policy. I am keen to learn about your experience; what you see as the key factors of policy success or failure at different stages of the policymaking process. I will draw on your responses in a generalised way. Comments you make may be used in the analysis but no comments or statements in the thesis will be attributed to you, nor will you be identifiable from the comments used in either my thesis, or any other publications arising from this research.'

To start with, could you run me through your experience in environment policy – how long you have worked in the area and what policies or programs you have had a direct role in developing or managing?

- Which federal environment policies or programs do you think have been particularly successful?

- What are the key factors that need to be in place to achieve a successful environment policy?

- What in your experience are some of the primary barriers to achieving successful environment policy?

Specific policy experiences:

I would like to talk to you about your experiences in the policy development process. You might like to refer to one or more specific environment policies or programs you had a direct role in or you may wish to respond more broadly.

- What was the policy initiative?

- What was your specific role?

- In your view was the policy successfully implemented? Why/why not?

- Could you take me through the policy process? What happened?

- Looking back, do you think you had a prior sense that the policy might succeed or fail? If so, why? If so, were your intuitions right or wrong? Were you able to inject your intuitions into the policy process?

- Were there any signals or flags early in the process that the policy or program would work?

- Can you provide or point me to any documents relevant to the particular policy we are discussing?

- Do you know where the policy came from – how it got on the Government's agenda?

- Were the policy objectives clear? What was the primary objective? Were there other/secondary objectives?

- What was the process to design the policy? Were different options discussed and assessed? Why was the particular design of the policy selected? What influenced this?

- What role did evidence play in the process?

- What involvement did external stakeholders have, if any, in the policy idea and the design?

- How significant was the role of the central agencies (PM&C, Treasury, Finance)? In what way? Did they have a direct hand in steering the process, in setting objectives?

- Are you currently involved in any emerging environment policies? If so, what are the main factors in your view likely to impact on a successful outcome for that policy?

Broader policy issues:

- We have been talking about policymaking – and the factors involved in policy success or failure. How would you define policy? How would you define policy success in the environment context?

- Some policy theorists hold that the skills and experience of particular individual public servants are a key to whether a policy can be successfully delivered. What is your view?

- Drawing on your experiences, if you had to identify three lessons for new graduates in how to craft environment policies that succeed, what would you say?

- Do you think the making of environment policy faces different challenges from other federal policy areas (such as employment, health, education)? If so, why?

- Do you have any other comments on environment policymaking you would like to add?

Agreement to use the material in the interview (non-identified) _____

Consent form signed _____

Respondent Profile:

Current or former _____

M or F _____

Years of involvement in environment policy _____

Years of involvement in other (non-environment) policy _____

Level _____

Central agency experience _____

Direct experience in a minister's office _____

References

ABC News. 3 April 2010. Tony Burke made first Population Minister. http://www.abc.net.au/news/2010-04-03/tony-burke-made-first-population-minister/390256 [Accessed September 2015]

ABC News. 14 April 2010. New survey shows hostility towards a Big Australia. http://www.abc.net.au/am/content/2010/s2872072.htm [Accessed September 2015]

ABC News. 16 May 2011. National Population Strategy launched on the Gold Coast. http://www.abc.net.au/news/2011-05-13/national-population-strategy-launched-on-the-gold/2715178 [Accessed September 2015]

ABC News. 5 June 2015. Olive Vale: Queensland Government asks Commonwealth to stop bulldozers clearing land on Cape York property. http://www.abc.net.au/news/2015-06-04/queensland-government-steps-in-to-stop-olive-vale-land-clearing/6521928 [Accessed December 2015]

ABC News. 5 May 2017. Dodo's relative, Nicobar pigeon, found in north-west Australia's Kimberley region. http://www.abc.net.au/news/2017-05-05/dodo-relative-nicobar-pigeon-found-in-north-west-australia/8500442 [Accessed July 2017]

ABC Radio National. 16 March 2014. The trouble with offsets. *Background Briefing.*

Advisory Group on Reform of Australian Government Administration. 2010. *Ahead of the Game: Blueprint for the Reform of Australian Government Administration.* Canberra: Commonwealth of Australia.

Ajani, J. 2007. *The Forest Wars.* Carlton, Victoria: MUP.

Allen, L. 3 July 2017. Australia doesn't have a population policy – why. *The Conversation.* https://theconversation.com/australia-doesnt-have-a-population-policy-why-78183 [Accessed July 2017]

Allen Consulting Group. 2011. *Assessment of the economic and employment outcomes of the Working on Country program, Report to the Department of Sustainability, Environment, Water, Population and Communities.* Canberra: Allen Consulting Group.

Althaus, C. 2004. Policy Design and the Calculation of Political Risk. PhD, Griffith University.

Althaus, C. 2008. *Calculating Political Risk.* Sydney: UNSW Press.

Althaus, C., Bridgman, P. & G. Davis. 2007. *The Australian Policy Handbook.* Sydney: Allen and Unwin.

Altman, J. and F. Markham. 2013. Submission into the House of Representatives Standing Committee on Aboriginal and Torres Strait Islander Affairs Inquiry into the Native Title Amendment Bill 2012. ANU: Centre for Aboriginal Economic Policy Research.

ANAO. 2006. *Implementation of Programme and Policy Initiatives: Making Implementation Matter. Better Practice Guide*. Canberra: ANAO.

ANAO. 2010. *Home Insulation Program, Audit Report No. 12 2010-11, Performance Audit*. Canberra: ANAO.

ANAO. 2011. *Indigenous Employment in Government Service Delivery Audit Report No. 4 2011-12*. Canberra: ANAO.

Architecture and Design. 2011. Population policy gains mixed response. http://www.architectureanddesign.com.au/news/industry-news/population-policy-gains-mixed-response [Accessed September 2015]

Australian Financial Review. 7 October 2015. Costly education mess is ended. [Editorial]

Australian Government. 2015. *Our North, Our Future: White Paper on Developing Northern Australia*. Canberra: Australian Government.

Australian Government. 2017. *Australia State of the Environment 2016: Overview*. Canberra: Australian Government.

Australian Public Service Commission. 2015. Capability Review Program. http://www.apsc.gov.au/priorities/capability-reviews [Accessed November 2015]

Australian Royal Commission into the Home Insulation Program. 2014a. *Report of the Royal Commission into the Home Insulation Program*. Canberra: Commonwealth of Australia.

Australian Royal Commission into the Home Insulation Program. 2014b. Transcript of Proceedings. Brisbane: Commonwealth of Australia.

Bachelard, M., Cook, H., and M. Knott. 16 September 2015. Vocational education, the biggest get-rich quick scheme in Australia. *Sydney Morning Herald*.

Banks, G. 2009. Evidence-based policy-making: What is it? How do we get it? *Public Administration Today*. (Oct-Dec): 9-23.

Banks, G. 2013. Restoring Trust in Public Policy: What Role for the Public Service? *Garran Oration for the IPAA. November 21*.

Bardach, E. 2009. *A Practical Guide for Policy Analysis: the Eightfold Path to More Effective Problem Solving*. Washington, DC: CQ Press.

Barrett, S. & C. Fudge (eds). 1981. *Policy and Action*. London: Methuen.

Barrett, S. M. 2004. Implementation studies: Time for a revival? Personal reflections on 20 years of implementation studies. *Public Administration*. 82 (3) 249-262.

Baumgartner, F. & B. Jones. 2009. *Agendas and Instability in American Politics.* Chicago: University of Chicago Press.

Beder, S. 2002. *Global spin: the corporate assault on environmentalism.* Revised edition. Foxhole, Dartington, Totnes, Devon: Green Books.

Bennet, J. 2015. We need an energy miracle. *The Atlantic.* November.

Betts, K. 13 March 2015. The tenuous link between population and prosperity. *The Conversation.* http://theconversation.com/the-tenuous-link-between-population-and-prosperity-38291[Accessed September 2015]

Betts, K. 2015. *Voters' attitudes to population growth in Australia: results of a survey conducted for Sustainable Population Australia.* The Australian Population Research Institute, Monash University: Clayton, Victoria.

Betts, K. & B. Birrell. 2017. *Australian voters' views on immigration policy.* The Australian Population Research Institute, Monash University: Clayton, Victoria.

Boaz, A. & R. Pawson. 2005. The perilous road from evidence to policy: five journeys compared. *Journal of Social Policy.* 34 (2): 175-194.

Böhm, S. 12 April 2013. Why are carbon markets failing? *The Guardian.*

Bongiorno, F. 2015. *The Eighties: The Decade that Transformed Australia.* Collingwood, Victoria: Black Inc.

Bourke, L. 24 February, 2017. Sydney has the second least affordable housing in the world. *Sydney Morning Herald.*

Bryman, A. 2008. *Social Research Methods.* Oxford: Oxford University Press.

Bullock, H., Mountford, J. & R. Stanley. 1999. *Better Policy Making.* Centre for Management and Policy Studies, London: The Cabinet Office.

Burgess, C. P., Johnston, F. H., Berry, H. L., McDonnell, J., Yibarbuk, D., Gunabarra, C., Mileran, A. & R.S. Bailie. 2009. Healthy country, healthy people: the relationship between Indigenous health status and "caring for country". *Medical Journal of Australia.* 190 (10): 567-572.

Caring for our Country Review Team. 2012. *Caring for our Country: Report of the Review of the Caring for our Country Initiative.* Canberra: Australian Government.

Carrington, D. 26 September 2014. World population to hit 11bn in 2100: New study overturns 20 years of consensus. *Guardian Weekly.* Manchester: DNM Limited.

Carson, R. 1962. *Silent Spring.* Boston: Houghton Mifflin.

Castles, S. 2004. Why migration policies fail. *Ethnic and Racial Studies.* 27 (2): 205-227.

Climate Change Authority (CCA). 2014. *Light Vehicle Emissions Standards for Australia: Research Report.* Melbourne: CCA.

Colebatch, H. K. 1998. *Policy.* Buckingham: Open University Press.

Colebatch, H. K. 2007. The work of policy, the work of analysis. *Public Policy Network Conference.* Adelaide February 2007.

Colebatch, H. K., Hoppe, R. & M. Noordegraff (eds). 2010. *Working for Policy.* Amsterdam: Amsterdam University Press.

Commonwealth of Australia. 1992. *National Strategy for Ecologically Sustainable Development.* Canberra: Australian Government.

Commonwealth of Australia. 2010. *Intergenerational Report 2010.* Canberra: Australian Government.

Commonwealth of Australia. Senate. Environment, Communications, and the Arts References Committee. 2010. Inquiry into the Energy Efficient Homes Package ('ceiling insulation'). Canberra: Australian Government.

Commonwealth of Australia. 2011. *Sustainable Australia Sustainable Communities – A Sustainable Population Strategy for Australia.* Canberra: Australian Government.

Commonwealth of Australia. 2015a. *Budget Paper No. 3.* Canberra: Australian Government.

Commonwealth of Australia. 2015b. *2015 Intergenerational Report 2010: Australia in 2055.* Canberra: Australian Government.

Commonwealth of Australia. 2016. *Budget Paper No. 3.* Canberra: Australian Government.

Commonwealth of Australia. 2017. *Budget Paper No. 3.* Canberra: Australian Government.

Costello, P. 1 November 2013. Personal communication to Dr D. Meacheam, at UNSW Canberra.

Crace, L. 2011. The fallout to the guide to the proposed basin plan. *Australian Journal of Public Administration.* 70 (1): 84-93.

Crowley, K. 2002. Environmental policy. *In*: Summers, J., Woodward, D. and A. Parkin (eds.). *Government, Politics, Power and Policy in Australia.* 7th ed. NSW: Pearson Education Australia.

Crowley, K. & K. Walker (eds.). 2012. *Environmental Policy Failure: the Australian Story.* Prahran, Victoria: Tilde University Press.

Davis, G., Wanna, J., Warhurst, J. & P. Weller. 1993. *Public Policy in Australia.* St Leonards, NSW: Allen & Unwin.

Denniss, R. 5 March 2015. Hockey's IGR meaningless forecasts based on magical thinking. *Crikey.* http://www.crikey.com.au/2015/03/05/hockeys-igr-meaningless-forecasts-based-on-magical-thinking/ [Accessed September 2015]

Denzin, N. K. & Y. S. Lincoln (eds.). 2003. *Strategies of Qualitative Inquiry.* Thousand Oaks, California: Sage Publications.

Department of Environment and Heritage. 2004. History of the Department of the Environment and Heritage. Canberra: Commonwealth of Australia.

Department of Environment Water Heritage and the Arts. 2009. Submission to the Senate Enquiry into the Energy Efficient Homes Package.

Department of Environment Water Heritage and the Arts. 2010a. *Annual Report 2009-10*. Commonwealth of Australia.

Department of Environment Water Heritage and the Arts. 2010b. *Australia's Biodiversity Conservation Strategy 2010-2030*. Canberra: Australian Government.

Department of Immigration and Border Protection. 2015. 2013-14 Migration Progamme Report. http://www.border.gov.au/ReportsandPublications/Documents/statistics/report-migration-programme-2013-14.pdf [Accessed September 2015]

Department of Industry and Science. 2015. Home Insulation Program Industry Payment Scheme. http://www.industry.gov.au/industry/IndustryInitiatives/Home-Insulation-Program-Industry-Payment-Scheme/Pages/default.aspx [Accessed September 2015]

Department of Sustainability Environment Water Population and Communities (DSEWPAC). 2010. *A sustainable population strategy for Australia: issues paper and appendices*. Canberra: Commonwealth of Australia.

Department of Sustainability Environment Water Population and Communities (DSEWPAC). 2011a. Analysis of performance of the Working on Country program: Final Report. Canberra: Unpublished.

Department of Sustainability Environment Water Population and Communities (DSEWPAC). 2011b. *State of the Air in Australia 1999-2008.* Canberra: Commonwealth of Australia.

Department of Sustainability Environment Water Population and Communities (DSEWPAC). 2012. Fact Sheet: Working on Country. Canberra: Commonweatlh of Australia.

Department of Sustainability Environment Water Population and Communities (DSEWPAC). 2013. *Annual Report 2012-13*. Canberra: Commonwealth of Australia.

Department of Sustainability Environment Water Population and Communities (DSEWPAC). June 2013. Working on Country: Reporting back to you: 2009-2012 Report to Working on Country funded recipients. Canberra: Commonwealth of Australia.

Department of the Environment. 2013a. *About the EPBC Act* [Online]. Canberra: Commonwealth of Australia. http://www.environment.gov.au/topics/about-us/legislation/environment-protection-and-biodiversity-conservation-act-1999/about-epbc [Accessed November 2013].

Department of the Environment. 2013b. *Annual Reports* [Online]. Available: http://www.environment.gov.au/topics/about-us/accountability-reporting/annual-reports [Accessed October 2013].

Department of the Environment. 2014. *One-stop shop approved by Government.* [Online]. Available: http://www.environment.gov.au/minister/hunt/2013/mr20131016.html [Accessed March 2014]

Department of the Environment. 2015a. Fuel quality standards. http://www.environment.gov.au/topics/environment-protection/fuel-quality/standards [Accessed September 2015]

Department of the Environment. 2015b. Have your say on a sustainable population strategy for Australia – issues report released. http://environment.gov.au/minister/archive/burke/2010/mr20101216.html [Accessed July 2015]

Department of the Environment. 2015c. Public Consultations: Submissions to a Sustainable Population Strategy for Australia. http://secure.environment.gov.au/sustainability/population/consultation/index.html [Accessed December 2015]

Department of the Environment 2015d. Sustainable population. http://www.environment.gov.au/topics/sustainable-communities/sustainable-population [Accessed September 2015]

Department of the Environment and Water Resources. 2007. Working on Country Programme 2007-2008 Application Guidelines. Canberra: Australian Government.

Di Muzio, T. 2015. *The 1% and the rest of us.* London: Zed Books.

Dovers, S. 2005. *Environment and Sustainability Policy: Creation, Implementation and Evaluation.* Australia: The Federation Press.

Dovers, S. 2013. The Australian environment policy agenda. *Australian Journal of Public Administration.* 72 (2): 114-128.

Dovers, S. & K. Hussey. 2013. *Environment and Sustainability: a Policy Handbook.* Federation Press. 2nd edition.

Downs, A. 1972. Up and down with ecology: The issue attention cycle. *Public Interest.* (28): 38-50.

Dryzek, J. 1987. *Rational Ecology: Environment and Political Economy.* Oxford: Basil Blackwell Inc.

Dye, T. 2008. *Understanding Public Policy.* New Jersey: Pearson Prentice Hall.

Early, G. 2008. Australia's national environmental legislation and human/wildlife interactions. *Journal of International Wildlife Law and Policy.* 11 (2): 101-155.

Economou, N. 1999. Backwards into the future: national policy making, devolution and the rise and fall of the environment. *In:* Walker, K. and K. Crowley (eds.). *Australian Environment Policy 2: Issues in Decline and Devolution.* Sydney: UNSW Press.

Edwards, M. 2001. Participatory Governance into the Future: Roles of the Government and Community Sectors. *Australian Journal of Public Administration.* 60 (3): 78-88.

Environment Australia. 2000. *Summary Report of the Review of Fuel Quality Requirements for Australian Transport.* Canberra: Australian Government.

Environment Australia. 2001. *Stakeholder Consultation and Scenario Development: Review of Fuel Quality Report.* Canberra: Australian Government.

Essential Media. 4 October 2016. *The Essential Report: 4 October 2016. http://www.essentialvision.com.au/ wp-content/uploads/2016/10/Essential-Report_161004.pdf* [Accessed October 2016]

Feldman, M. 1989. *Order without Design: Information Production and Policy Making.* Stanford, California: Stanford University Press.

Ferraro, S. Vehicle emissions standards: why Australia needs them and why they're NOT a carbon tax. 13 July 2017. *RenewEconomy.* https://reneweconomy.com.au/vehicle-emissions-standards-why-australia-needs-them-and-why-theyre-not-a-carbon-tax-42159/ [Accessed July 2017]

Fitzsimons, J., Legge, S., Traill, B. & J. Woinarski (eds.). 2010. *Into Oblivion? The Disappearing Native Mammals of Northern Australia.* Melbourne: The Nature Conservancy.

Freiberg, A. & W. G. Carson. 2010. The limits to evidence-based policy: evidence, emotion and criminal justice. *Australian Journal of Public Administration.* 69 (2): 152–164.

Garnett, S. T. & B. Sithole. 2007. *Sustainable Northern Landscapes and the Nexus with Indigenous Health: Healthy Country Healthy People.* Canberra: Land and Water Australia.

Goodin, R. 1982. *Political Theory and Public Policy.* Chicago: University of Chicago Press.

Great Britain Cabinet Office. 1999a. Modern Policy-Making: Ensuring Policies Deliver Value for Money. Report by the Comptroller and Auditor General. London: National Audit Office.

Great Britain Cabinet Office. 1999b. *Professional Policy Making for the Twenty First Century: Report by the Strategic Policy Making Team.* London: The Cabinet Office.

Greenhalgh, T. & J. Russell. 2009. Evidence-based policymaking: a critique. *Perspectives in Biology and Medicine.* 52 (2): 304-318.

Grindle, M. 1981. Anticipating failure: the implementation of rural development programs. *Public Policy.* 29 (1): 51-74.

Harmelink, M., Nilsson, L. & R. Harmsen. 2008. Theory-based evaluation of 20 energy efficiency instruments. *Energy Efficiency,* 1 (2): 131-148.

Hartcher, P. 2011. *The sweet spot: how Australia made its own luck and could now throw it all away.* Collingwoood, Vic: Black Inc.

Hartcher, P. 1 September 2015. 'Police or perish' gets some big muscle. *Sydney Morning Herald.*

Hart Energy. 2014. *International Fuel Quality Standards and Their Implications for Australian Standards.* Houston: Hart Energy.

Hawke, A. 2009. *The Australian Environment Act. Report of the Independent Review of the Environment Protection and Biodiversity Conservation Act 1999: Final Report.* Canberra: DEWHA.

Hawke, A. 2010. *Review of the Administration of the Home Insulation Program.* Canberra: Australian Government.

Head, B. W. 2008. Three lenses of evidence-based policy. *Australian Journal of Public Administration.* 67 (1): 1-11.

Higgs, K. 2014. *Collision course: endless growth on a finite planet.* Cambridge, Mass.: MIT Press.

Hindmoor, A. & A. McConnell. 2013. Why didn't they see it coming? Warning signs, acceptable risks and the Global Financial Crisis. *Political Studies.* 61 (3): 543-560.

Hogwood, B. W. & L.A. Gunn. 1984. *Policy Analysis for the Real World.* Oxford: Oxford University Press.

Howlett, M. 2009. Policy analytical capacity and evidence-based policy-making: Lessons from Canada. *Canadian Public Administration.* 52 (2): 153-175.

Howlett, M., Ramesh, M. & A. Perl. 2009. *Studying Public Policy: Policy Cycles and Policy Subsystems.* Ontario: Oxford University Press.

Hunt, G. The Hon. MP. 6 March 2014. Media Release: Approval of grazing trial in the Wonnangatta Valley. [Online] [Accessed May 2014]

Hunt, G. The Hon. MP. 15 October 2015. Media Release: Carmichael Coal Mine and Rail Infrastructure Project. [Online] [Accessed December 2017]

Institute of Public Administration Australia (IPAA). April 2012. Public Policy Drift: Why governments must replace 'policy on the run' and 'policy by fiat' with a 'business case' approach to regain public confidence, Public Policy Discussion Paper. Sydney: IPAA.

Kanyirninpa Jukurrpa. 2013. *Annual Report 2013.* Newman, WA: Kanyirninpa Jukurrpa.

Keeffe, K. 2014. *Statement of Witness* [Online]. Available: http://www.homeinsulationroyalcommission.gov.au/Hearings/Documents/Evidence31March2014/STA.001.015.0001.pdf [Accessed April 2014]

Kellow, A. 2009. Environmental politics. *In:* Rhodes, R.A.W. (ed.). *The Australian Study of Politics.* London: Palgrave Macmillan.

Kingdon, J. 2003. *Agendas, Alternatives and Public Policies.* New York: Longman.

Kingdon, J. 2011. *Agendas, Alternatives and Public Policies.* Boston: Longman (Updated second edition).

Kortt, M. A. & B. Dollery. 2012. The Home Insulation Program: An example of Australian Government failure. *Australian Journal of Public Administration.* 71 (1): 65-75.

Kraft, M. E. & S. R. Furlong. 2010. *Public Policy: Politics, Analysis and Alternative.* Washington DC: CQ Press.

Krien, A. 2010. *Into the Woods: The Battle for Tasmania's Forests.* Collingwood, Victoria: Black Inc.

Krockenberger, M. 2015. *Population Growth in Australia.* Canberra: The Australia Institute.

Lasswell, H.D. 1956. *The Decision Process: Seven Categories of Functional Analysis.* College Park: University of Maryland Press.

Lewis, C. 2010. The Home Insulation Program policy debacle: haste makes waste. *Public Policy.* 5 (2): 83-100.

Lindblom, C. 1959. The science of muddling through. *Public Administration Review.* 19 (3): 79-88.

Lindblom, C. 1979. Still muddling through. *Public Administration Review.* 36 (6): 517-526.

Lindenmayer, D. 2007. *On Borrowed Time: Australia's Environmental Crisis and What We Must Do About It.* Camberwell, Victoria: Penguin Group and CSIRO Publishing.

Linder, S. H. & B.G. Peters. 1987. A design perspective on policy implementation: the fallacies of misplaced prescription. *Policy Studies Review.* 6 (3): 459-475.

Lipsky, M. 1980. *Street-Level Bureaucracy: The Dilemmas of Individuals in the Public Service.* New York: Russell Sage Foundation.

Local Court of NSW Coronial Jurisdiction. 4 October 2012. Inquest into the death of Marcus Wilson. Sydney: State Coroner's Court, Glebe.

Mackay, K. 2004. Two Generations of Performance Evaluation and Management Systems in Australia. *ECD Working Paper Series, No. 11*. Washington DC: World Bank.

Mackie, K. 2015. Federal environment policymaking in Australia: avoiding failure; pursuing success. PhD, UNSW.

Maddison, S. & R. Denniss. 2009. *An Introduction to Australian Public Policy: Theory and Practice*. Port Melbourne, Victoria: Cambridge University Press.

Markus, A. *Mapping Social Cohesion 2016: The Scanlon Foundation Surveys Report*. 2016. Melbourne: Scanlon Foundation, Australian Multicultural Foundation, Monash University.

Markus, A. *Mapping Social Cohesion 2017: The Scanlon Foundation Surveys Report*. 2017. Melbourne: Scanlon Foundation, Australian Multicultural Foundation, Monash University.

Marsden Jacob Associates. 2015. *Independent Review of the Fuel Quality Standards Act 2000: Issues Paper*. Melbourne: Marsden Jacob Associates.

Marsden Jacob Associates. 2016. *Final Report: Review of the Fuel Quality Standards Act 2000*. Melbourne: Marsden Jacob Associates.

Marsh, D. & A. McConnell. 2010. Towards a framework for establishing policy success. *Public Administration*. 88 (2) 564-583.

Marsten, G. & R. Watts. 2003. Tampering with the evidence: a critical appraisal of evidence-based policy-making. *The Drawing Board: An Australian Review of Public Affairs*. 3 (3): 143-163.

Mayntz, R. 1983. The conditions of effective public policy: a new challenge for policy analysis. *Policy and Politics*. 11 (2): 123-143.

Mazmanian, D. & P. Sabatier. 1983. *Implementation and public policy*. Glenview: Scott.

McConnell, A. 2010a. Policy success, policy failure and grey areas in-between. *Journal of Public Policy*. 30 (3): 345-362.

McConnell, A. 2010b. *Understanding Policy Success: Rethinking Public Policy*. Basingstoke, Hampshire: Palgrave Macmillan.

McPhee, I. 2006. Evaluation and Performance Audit: Close cousins – or distant relatives? *Canberra Evaluation Forum*. Canberra.

Middle, G. J. 2010. Environmental Policy Making in Highly Contested Contexts: The success of adaptive-collaborative approaches. PhD, Curtin University of Technology.

Milman, O. & N. Evershed. 12 August 2015. Australia has denied environmental approval to just 18 projects since 2000. *Guardian Australia.*

Monash University. 2015. Population Growth. http://monash.edu/mapping-population/public-opinion/surveys/inventory-of-surveys/population.html [Accessed July 2015]

Moran, M., Rein, M. & R. Goodin (eds). 2008. *The Oxford Handbook of Public Policy.* Oxford: Oxford University Press.

Moran, T. 2013. Reforming to Create Value: Our Next Five Strategic Steps. *Australian Journal of Public Administration.* 73 (2): 193-205.

National Environmental Protection Council (NEPM). 2011. *Ambient Air Quality NEPM Review.* Adelaide: NEPM. Sourced at http://www.scew.gov.au/resource/national-environment-protection-ambient-air-quality-measure-review-review-report.

Nevill, J. 2007. Policy failure: Australian freshwater protected area networks. *Australasian Journal of Environmental Management.* (1): 35-47.

Newman, J. 2014. Measuring Policy Success: Case Studies from Canada and Australia. *Australian Journal of Public Administration.* 73 (2): 192-205.

New York University. 2011. What is Research Design?, 2011. Available: www.nyu.edu/classes/bkg/methods/005847ch1.pdf.

New Zealand Labour. 2016. Making immigration work for New Zealand. http://www.labour.org.nz/immigration [Accessed December 2016]

Nowlin, M. C. 2011. Theories of the policy process: state of the research and emerging trends. *Policy Studies Journal.* 30 (S1): 41-60.

Nutley, S. 2003. Bridging the policy-research divide: reflections and lessons from the United Kingdom. *Canberra Bulletin of Public Administration.* (108): 19-28.

Nutley, S., Walter, I. & H. Davies. 2009. Past, present, and possible futures for evidence-based policy. *In*: Argyrous, G (ed.). *Evidence for policy and decision-making.* Sydney: UNSW Press.

O'Connor, M., Brown, J. & O. Hartwich. 2012. *Why vs Why: Big Australia.* Neutral Bay, NSW: Pantera Press.

O'Connor, M. & W.J. Lines. 2010. *Overloading Australia.* Canterbury NSW: Envirobook.

O'Toole, L. J., Jr. 2004. The theory-practice issue in policy implementation research. *Public Administration.* 82 (2): 309-329.

Office of the State Coroner. 4 July 2013. Inquest into the deaths of Matthew James FULLER, Rueben Kelly BARNES and Mitchell Scott SWEENEY. Brisbane: Queensland Courts.

Page, E. C. & B. Jenkins. 2005. *Policy Bureaucracy: Government with a Cast of Thousands.* Oxford: Oxford University Press.

Palmer, D. 2007. The Values Shaping Australian Asylum Policy: A Historical and Ethical Inquiry. PhD, UNSW.

Parliament of Australia. 18 October 2010. Environment and Communications Legislation Committee. Transcript at: http://parlinfo.aph.gov.au/parlInfo/search/display/display.w3p;query=Id%3A%22committees%2Festimate%2F13298%2F0003%22 [Accessed September 2015]

Parsons, W. 1995. *Public Policy: An Introduction to the Theory and Practice of Policy Analysis.* Cheltenham, UK: Edward Elgar Publishing.

Parsons, W. 2002. From muddling through to muddling up: evidence based policy making and the modernisation of British Government. *Public Policy and Administration.* 17 (3) 43-60.

Pearse, G. 2007. *High and Dry.* Victoria: Penguin.

Pew Charitable Trusts and Synergies Economic Consulting. 2015. *Working for our Country: A review of the economic and social benefits of indigenous land and sea management.* US: Pew Charitable Trusts.

Piketty, T. 2014. *Capital in the Twenty-First Century.* Cambridge: Harvard University Press.

Pollitt, C. & G. Bouchaert. 2011. *Public Management Reform: A Comparative Analysis. New Public Management, Governance and the Neo-Weberian State.* Oxford: Oxford University Press.

Pressman, J. L. & A. Wildavsky. 1973. *Implementation: how great expectations in Washington are dashed in Oakland; Or, Why it's amazing that federal programs work at all.* Berkeley, California: University of California Press.

Prime Minister. 3 February 2009a. Media release: $42 billion nation building and jobs plan.

Prime Minister. 3 February 2009b. Media Release: Energy Efficient Homes – Ceiling insulation in 2.7 million homes.

Pülzl , H. & O. Treib. 2007. Implementing public policy. *In:* Fischer, F., Miller, G. J. & M.S. Sidney (eds.). *Handbook of Public Policy Analysis.* Boca Raton: CRC Press.

Putnis, A., Josif, P. & E. Woodward. 2007. *Healthy Country Healthy People: Supporting Indigenous Engagement in the Sustainable Management of Northern Territory Land and Seas: A Strategic Framework.* Darwin: CSIRO.

Reich, R. B. 2015. *Saving Capitalism: For the Many, Not the Few*. New York: Knopf.

Rutter, J., Marshall, E. & S. Sims. 2012. *The "S" Factors: Lessons from the Institute for Government's policy success reunions*. UK: Institute for Government.

Sabatier, P (ed). 2007. *Theories of the policy process*. Boulder, Colorado: Westview.

Sabatier, P. & D. Mazmanian. 1979. The conditions of effective implementation. *Policy Analysis*. (5): 481-504.

Schneider, A. & H. Ingram. 1988. Systematically pinching ideas: a comparative approach to policy design. *Journal of Public Policy*. 8 (1): 61-80.

Schneider, A. & M. Sidney. 2009. What is next for policy design and social construction theory? *Policy Studies Journal*. 37: (1).

Schön, D. 1995. *The Reflexive Practitioner: how Professionals Think in Action*. England: Ashgate Publishing.

Schwartz-Shea, P. & D. Yanow. 2012. *Interpretive Research Design: Concepts and Processes*. New York: Routledge.

Shore, C. & S. Wright (eds). 1997. *Anthropology of Policy: Critical perspectives on governance and power*. Abington Oxon: Routledge.

Smith, D. 2009. Making management count: a case for theory and evidence-based public management. *Journal of Policy Analysis and Management*. 28 (1): 496-516.

Smyth, D. 2011a. Indigenous land and sea management. Report prepared for the Australian Government Department of Sustainability, Environment, Water, Population and Communities (DSEWPAC) on behalf of the State of the Environment 2011 Committee. Canberra: DSEWPAC.

Smyth, D. 2011b. *Review of Working on Country and Indigenous Protected Area Programs Through Telephone Interviews: Final report for the Department of Sustainability, Environment, Water, Population and Communities*. Atherton, Queensland: Smyth and Bahrdt Consultants.

Social Ventures Australia (SVA). 2014. *Social Return on Investment Report: Social, economic and cultural impact of Kanyirninpa Jukurrpa's On-Country programs*. Sydney: SVA.

State of the Environment 2011 Committee. 2011. *Australia State of the Environment 2011. Independent Report to the Australian Government Minister for Sustainability, Environment, Water, Population and Communities (DSEWPAC)*. Canberra: DSEWPAC.

Stewart, J. 2009. *Public Policy Values*. Hampshire, England: Palgrave Macmillan.

Stewart, J. & C. Hendriks. 2008. Discovering the environment. *In:* Aulich, C. & R. Wettenhall (eds.). *Howard's Fourth Government: Australian Commonwealth Administration 2004-2007*. Sydney: UNSW Press.

Stewart, J. & G. Jones. 2003. *Renegotiating the Environment: The Power of Politics.* Sydney: The Federation Press.

Stewart, J. & K. Mackie. 2011. When policy goes wrong: the problem of transmitted risk. *Australian Journal of Political Science.* 46 (4): 669-682.

Stoker, G. 1998. Governance as theory: five propositions. *International Social Science Journal.* 50 (155) 17-28.

Swan, W. April 9-10, 2011. How past saved nation's future: Swift action and lessons from the Great Depression protected Australia from the worst of the global economic crisis. *Sydney Morning Herald.*

't Hart, P. 2007. Review of Policy Bureaucracy: Government with a Cast of Thousands by Edward C. Page and Bill Jenkins. *Public Administration.* 84 (3): 783-810.

Thomas, I. 2007. *Environmental Policy: Australian Practice in the Context of Theory.* Sydney: The Federation Press.

Tiffen, R. 26 March 2010. A mess? A shambles? A disaster? Available: http://inside.org.au/a-mess-a-shambles-a-disaster/ [Accessed June 2013].

Tingle, L. 2015. *Political Amnesia: How we Forgot to Govern.* Quarterly Essay No. 60. Melbourne: Penguin.

Tingle, L. 21 July 2017. Immigration: a subject so scary that Turnbull hid it. *Australian Financial Review.*

Towell, N. 27 July 2013. Challenges in a changing world. *The Canberra Times.*

United Nations Development Programme (UNDP). 2015. *Post-2015 Sustainable Development Agenda.* New York: UNDP.

Urbanalyst. 2011. Population strategy released for Australia. http://www.urbanalyst.com/in-the-news/australia/591-population-strategy-released-for-australia.html [Accessed September 2015]

Urbis. 2012. *Assessment of the Social Outcomes of the Working on Country Program.* Australia: Urbis.

Van Assche, K., Beunen, R. & M. Duineveld. 2011. Performing success and failure in governance: Dutch planning experiences. *Public Administration.* 90 (3): 567-581.

Walker, K. (ed.). 1992. *Australian Environmental Policy.* Sydney: NSW University Press Ltd.

Walker, K. 1994. *The Political Economy of Environmental Policy: An Australian Introduction.* Sydney: UNSW Press.

Walker, K. and K. Crowley (eds). 1999. *Australian Environmental Policy 2: Studies in Decline and Devolution.* Sydney: UNSW Press.

WalterTurnbull. 2010. *Working on Country Evaluation Report to Department of the Environment, Water, Heritage and the Arts*. Canberra: Department of the Environment, Water, Heritage and the Arts.

Weimer, D. L. & A.R. Vining. 2005. *Policy Analysis: Concepts and Practice*. New Jersey: Pearson Prentice Hall.

Wescott, G. 2009. *Back to Basics: Breakthrough Proposals for the Australian Environment*. Sydney: UNSW Press.

Wildavsky, A. 1979. *The Art and Craft of Policy Analysis*. London and Basingstoke: The Macmillan Press.

Williams, A. 2010. Is evidence-based policymaking really possible? Reflections for policymakers and academics on making use of research in the work of policy. *In:* Colebatch, H., Hoppe, R. & M. Noordegraff (eds.). *Working for Policy*. Amsterdam: Amsterdam University Press.

Winter, S. C. 2007. Implementation Perspectives: Status and Recognition. *In:* Peters, G., B & J. Pierre (eds). *Handbook of Public Administration*. London: Sage Publications Ltd.

Yanow, D. 1996. *How does a Policy Mean? Interpreting Policy and Organisational Actions*. Washington DC: Georgetown University Press.

Yencken, D. & D. Wilkinson. 2000. *Resetting the Compass: Australia's Journey Towards Sustainability*. Collingwood, Victoria: CSIRO Publishing.

www.ingramcontent.com/pod-product-compliance
Lightning Source LLC
Chambersburg PA
CBHW080925050426
42334CB00056B/2938